HOW REASON CAN LEAD TO GOD

A PHILOSOPHER'S BRIDGE TO FAITH

JOSHUA RASMUSSEN

InterVarsity Press
P.O. Box 1400, Downers Grove, IL 60515-1426
ivpress.com
email@ivpress.com

InterVarsity Press® is the book-publishing division of InterVarsity Christian Fellowship/USA®, a movement of students and faculty active on campus at hundreds of universities, colleges, and schools of nursing in the United States of America, and a member movement of the International Fellowship of Evangelical Students. For information about local and regional activities, visit intervarsity.org.

Cover design: David Fassett
Interior design: Daniel van Loon
Image: silhouette head: © CSA Images / Getty Images

ISBN 978-0-8308-5252-9 (print)
ISBN 978-0-8308-6642-7 (digital)

Printed in the United States of America ♾

InterVarsity Press is committed to ecological stewardship and to the conservation of natural resources in all our operations. This book was printed using sustainably sourced paper.

Library of Congress Cataloging-in-Publication Data

Names: Rasmussen, Joshua L., author.
Title: How reason can lead to God : a philosopher's bridge to faith / Joshua Rasmussen.
Description: Downers Grove : InterVarsity Press, 2019. | Includes bibliographical references and index.
Identifiers: LCCN 2019013200 (print) | LCCN 2019019825 (ebook) | ISBN 9780830866427 (eBook) | ISBN 9780830852529 (pbk. : alk. paper)
Subjects: LCSH: Faith and reason—Christianity.
Classification: LCC BT50 (ebook) | LCC BT50 .R265 2019 (print) | DDC 210—dc23
LC record available at https://lccn.loc.gov/2019013200

P 27 26 25 24 23 22 21 20 19 18 17 16 15 14 13 12 11 10 9 8 7
Y 39 38 37 36 35 34 33 32 31 30 29 28 27 26 25 24 23

FOR MY SKEPTICAL FRIENDS

CONTENTS

PREFACE

I write for a specific sort of person. You value reason, science, and independent thinking. You question beliefs propped up by "faith" without sufficient evidence. Maybe you would like your life to have a deeper purpose, but you cannot believe something based on a mere wish. Whether you are a student, an academic, or just a curious person, you want one thing: the *truth*. If you can relate, this book is for you.

You might worry that this book is not about truth, not really. From the title, you might wonder whether I might be trying to use reason to rationalize a prior conclusion. Am I trying to contort "truth" to fit with my convictions? Am I interested in facing reality, even if it contradicts my desires or existing framework? Am I willing to be wrong? If you have these questions, this book is especially for you. I want you to ask these questions. They are the mark of an explorer. They are the questions that sparked my own journey, which ultimately led me to write this book.

I want this book to serve you no matter what perspective you come from. My purpose is not to knock you over with arguments or to suggest that you can only be rational if you agree with my viewpoint. Instead, I want to share with you some of the steps in my own journey in the hope that those steps may encourage you in yours.

My reason for writing this book is to mark out a pathway, step by step, that can inspire a greater vision of the ultimate *foundation* of everything. I begin with a story of my own journey. Then I begin the project of constructing a *bridge of reason* for your examination and exploration.

In the final chapters, I examine common questions about evil and suffering that can present obstacles to the destination.

While our inquiry will reach to the deepest layer of reality, I aim to make this book as readable as I can. Thus, I seek to replace all technical jargon with commonsense definitions in ordinary language. I never rest an argument on scholarly authority. Instead, I use the instruments of reason and common experience to serve you in your quest.

In my effort to maximize the value of this bridge, I follow three construction rules:

Rule 1. Make it inclusive: use materials—reason and experience—that are accessible to a wide audience, so you can check each piece.

Rule 2. No guessing: build each part on principles that you can *see* to be true.

Rule 3. Aim to serve: make a bridge that you can make your own—to analyze, reorganize, and build upon further.

Enjoy the journey.

ACKNOWLEDGMENTS

I am grateful for the invaluable feedback from many readers of earlier drafts. Thank you, especially, to Annesley DeHaven, Marc Dragoo, Jonathan Casad, Tyron Goldschmidt, Alan Leahy, Mila Lucia, David McNutt, Samuel Peterson, Charles Rasmussen, Jennifer Rasmussen, Joseph Schmid, Jared Brandon, Cameron Bertuzzi, Graham Oppy, and Justin Stewart. Special thanks goes to my wife, Rachel, who brought her own touch of wisdom and beauty to every chapter.

CHAPTER 1

WHEN REASON LEADS TO DOUBT

SEEDS OF DOUBT

From as early as I can remember, I have felt drawn to question things. When I was in second grade, I recall imagining that my classmates were fictional characters invented by aliens. I wondered how I could know for *sure* my friends were real, like me. Some nights I would lie in bed thinking about my questions. How can numbers go on forever? What happens if I travel back in time and stop myself from travelling back in time?

In my late teens, however, someone else's questions led me to questions I had never considered before. It started in a biology class. The questions that turned my mind were not about biological evolution. Rather, I met someone who didn't believe in any ultimate purpose. For the first time, I began to question the origin of everything.

As I talked with my non-believing friend, it became evident to me that he was sincere in his questions. He didn't appear to be trying to hide from a cosmic authority. In fact, he said he wished he could believe in a benevolent being who governs the world. His only problem, he said, was that he didn't have a sufficient reason to believe. He seemed nice and thoughtful.

I tried out a few arguments. In one argument, I asked him about the cause of the Big Bang. I proposed that there would need to be something that caused the first events. He seemed relaxed and curious as he listened to my argument. He then replied with questions. None of my arguments answered his root concerns.

After those initial conversations, a troubling question entered my mind: "Why wouldn't a perfectly loving being make its existence more obvious to my classmate?" Until then, I felt secure in the basic framework I knew from childhood. It made sense to me that meaning and purpose filled the universe. This "purpose-filled" understanding of things colored the background of my mind like a blue sky.

Yet my conversations with my friend caused that background to darken. More questions came like a flood. I wondered why news of the "right" religion is restricted to certain cultures and times. I wondered how it can be fair for someone to be condemned for having wrong beliefs. I wondered why pain and death pervade the animal kingdom. I wondered why so many babies, who have done no wrong, die without having any chance to pass the "tests" of life.

My questions led to doubts. My doubts led to more questions.

I walked home from school feeling heavy. When I arrived home, I had no energy. I walked into my room and plopped onto my bed. I felt worried. I was worried that everything is ultimately meaningless.

Then, as I lay on my bed, I got an idea. I could ask for a sign. The idea sparked action. I whispered, "If you move my ceiling fan, I'll know you are there." I waited to see if the divine power I had believed in would respond.

Nothing happened.

My heart sank. I instinctively began to pray, "Please be real."

I stopped myself as I considered the irony of my prayer. No one can decide whether to be real. My prayer made no sense. I wanted someone to be real, but I was finding it impossible and dishonest to continue to believe that this someone was *actually* there.

As I continued to ponder my questions, I discovered a science documentary on the origin of the universe. I was curious to find out what the scientists had to say. Maybe they had an answer to my concern.

These scientists reminded me of my friend from school. They were thoughtful and curious. They were also skeptical of an ultimate purpose. They were especially skeptical of beliefs without evidence. One eminent scientist, Stephen Hawking, described the origin of the universe like the bottom surface of a sphere. "There is nothing beyond the universe," he said.[1]

After that documentary, I pondered an image in my mind. I imagined a balloon that represented the universe. I first imagined that the balloon contained everything that exists. I then considered an alternative: I imagined that something beyond the balloon produced it. Both pictures seemed possible. Maybe the universe is self-contained. That would be simpler than the alternative. But maybe it isn't self-contained. How could I know which picture of reality is correct? I saw no way.

Like my friend from school, I began to see that I lacked an adequate reason to believe in something greater beyond the universe. My belief in a cosmic purpose began to recede away. My blue sky became gray.

Although I didn't like the gray, I noticed that I could not simply *choose* the color of the sky. I could no more decide to keep my prior beliefs than I could decide to keep an ocean wave from rolling away. Reality is what it is. I couldn't just make it what I wanted it to be.

Everything began to look colorless—a meaningless blur. I felt alone.

I wanted to sleep, but instead I lay in bed as I imagined my death. My thoughts of nothingness plucked a chord in my heart. I tried again to imagine it. I imagined dying. Once dead, I would be completely gone, without any awareness. I would not even be aware of having no awareness. I would simply be absent forever. I would then remain absent. Never again would I regain any awareness of anything, *not ever*.

I wanted to fall asleep and then wake up with everything different. But the same austere reality greeted me in the morning. There was no sign of purpose. Just shapes upon shapes. I had to face reality *as it is*, not as I hoped it would be. There was no going back.

THE VALUE OF TRUTH-SEEKING

Many people live by inspiring ideas, like that your life matters, or that everything works out for the good. But how could I believe these things? My friend from biology class didn't. I contemplated the difference between hope and truth. The hopeful ideas began to seem *too good* to be true.

---

[1]See S. Hawking, *A Brief History of Time* (New York: Bantam, 1988), chap. 8.

I pictured masses of people who did not seek truth. These masses followed a leader. They believed what the leader told them to believe. The masses didn't seek truth for themselves. Instead, they sought other things: security, purpose, significance, love. They were not even willing to be wrong. Rather than face reality, they built a wall of protection around their leader. Meanwhile, their leader built a wall of protection around their beliefs.

I saw a few strange ones dance away from the masses. They would express curiosity to discover truth—whatever the truth might be. They didn't seem particularly focused on defending prior convictions. Instead, they were explorers. Rather than find security under the blankets of doctrine, they found pleasure in seeing more than they had. They were truth-seekers.

I began to see the contrast between seeking *truths* and seeking *treasures*. The truth is not always a treasure. The path to truth is not the same as the path to treasures. I can seek a treasure in vain because the treasure might not even exist. I considered the stakes: either my life will ultimately end in nothing, or there is more to life beyond the shifting of shapes. The second option felt like a treasure. But the first felt like it could be the sober truth.

As I felt this tension between truth and treasure, I saw—more like felt—something that would change the course of my life. I felt the value of truth. A thought echoed within the center of my heart: "Truth is what you want."

Slivers of courage began to emerge within me. I could now appreciate the questions my friend from biology class asked. I understood the source of his curiosity. I understood the bravery it took him to question foundational things. He had within him the value for truth. That same value emerged within me.

When I saw the value of truth, I also realized that *seeking* truth is the best way to get truth. If you want truth, aim for it. You are more likely to hit a target if you aim to hit the target than if you don't aim at it. If you want truth, seek truth.

Perhaps it is too obvious to mention that seeking truth is a first step to getting truth. Yet I noticed within me a pull to aim for other things. For example, at times I felt drawn to aim to keep previous beliefs. Even in graduate school, where the value of truth is highly advertised, I sometimes felt pressure to seek cleverness and independent thinking.

Though painful, the sharp conflict within me helped me see the treasure of truth itself. I wanted to believe in ultimate purpose. In fact, I recall feeling worried that I could be in big trouble for having the wrong beliefs about purpose. However, it was obvious to me that these motivations for belief did not aim at truth: to aim for comforting beliefs is not to aim for true beliefs.

As I pondered these things, I came to a decision. In a moment, I declared to the center of my being, "I will be a seeker of truth." I decided to follow reason and evidence wherever they might lead me. I became committed to doing my best to seek out the truths about everything that interested me.

My newfound awareness of the value of truth gave me a sense of freedom and responsibility. I felt free to question everything. I felt responsible to question everything. I realized the light of reason might lead me to a discomforting vision of reality. So be it. Truth would be my reward.

Around that time, I wrote a short story about a person on a boat. I described his adventures. This explorer decided to go out as far as he could to discover unknown lands. He would come back to offer reports. But he would not stay long. As he would go out again, some people would follow him a certain distance. Most of them did not travel far from the familiar. While many of his friends paused on local ports, the explorer moved out into thick fog. He had to keep going to fulfill his purpose: to see more than he had. He was an explorer.

TO THE EXPLORERS

This book is for explorers. If you can relate to my story of doubt and curiosity, I think you will especially appreciate the journey ahead.

Whatever your precise view, you are committed to facing reality as it actually is. You are committed to growing in your understanding of things. You care about testing your beliefs against the real world. You would rather stick out among the crowd than to follow others off a cliff. You want to align with reality, not to defend what others say you should believe.

It takes courage to follow evidence into unknown places. Perhaps people who claim to have truth have misjudged you. They have misunderstood your intentions. Perhaps you have felt the irony as those who claim to have truth fail to answer the questions that drive your search. They have labelled you "unsafe" and exiled you to the wilderness. This treatment is often the cost of being an explorer.

My desire is to offer something that will be of genuine value to you. Instead of playing a game of intellectual chess, my purpose in this book is to present, for your careful consideration, a set of steps I took in my own pursuit of a greater understanding of the foundation of existence.

IN PURSUIT OF TREASURE

My interest in truth led me to books. I first discovered books in my dad's library. Some of them were about *worldviews*—theories of everything. I was intrigued to discover systematic approaches to my questions. In one particular book, I discovered an argument about *causes* and *effects*.[2] I had heard of similar arguments before, but I had never before seen such a careful articulation.

Later, I went to a university library and checked out a stack of books. This stack included books by philosophers who argued that the world has no ultimate purpose. I read many such books with extreme interest. As I read, I took notes and reformulated the many arguments into my own words. I studied the arguments and their many forms from many angles. I also began developing my own arguments as a way to explore various implications further.

My studies led me to clues. Each clue inspired further investigation. My commitment to truth remained central.

In the course of my investigation, I began to see some things I had previously thought were impossible to see. My original vision of the world was too limited. My research helped me see that the world is far greater and more complex than I had imagined. I began to feel thankful that my childhood vision of reality was shattered, for it was too simple.

---

[2]One of the first books that took me deeper was Norman Geisler's *Philosophy of Religion*, 1st ed. (Grand Rapids: Baker Book House, 1974). Another helpful resource was William Rowe's *The Cosmological Argument* (Princeton: Princeton University Press, 1975).

Much later, it occurred to me that it takes courage not only to face cold truth, but it also takes courage to look for a treasure before you know whether the treasure is real. The risk is disappointment.

This book is about the search for a treasure. Many treasures are not obvious, but we can find them without leaping into the dark. In this book, I will attempt to construct a bridge of reason that can help truth-seekers explore a pathway to a valuable discovery.

You will be the judge. My goal is to bring you encouragement about the big picture of your life through the unalterable rules of reason. I invite you to put the bridge to the test. Without a rational basis for our steps, we walk blindly.

Reason will give us light.

CHAPTER 2

THE BRIDGE OF REASON

I will seek to build a bridge of reason that leads, step by step, to a special treasure. My building materials are planks of rational thought. I collected many of these materials from books and articles I read during my time of doubt and discovery (and beyond).[1] I have refined them and made them my own. This bridge is a modern design built with time-tested materials.

I do not wish to coerce anyone to cross my bridge unwillingly. Instead, I build this bridge to create an opportunity for explorers to explore. I invite you, then, to test each step carefully. Try to find holes in the bridge. Try to break it. Test its strength for yourself. You are the owner of this journey.

THE SCHEMATICS

Before I present the first step onto the bridge, it will help to have a picture of the basic design. I begin with the schematics. My construction tools are rules of logic. For example, I will use the law of non-contradiction:

---

[1]The materials span the philosophical landscape from Aristotle to current day philosophers. Some highlights include Aristotle, *Metaphysics*, trans. Joe Sachs (New Mexico City: Green Lion Press, 2002); D. Scotus, *Duns Scotus: Philosophical Writings* (Indianapolis: Hackett, 1987); T. Aquinas, *Summa Theologiae*, trans. Fathers of the English Dominican Province (New York: Benzinger, 1948); G. Leibniz, "On the Ultimate Origin of Things," in *Discourse on Metaphysics and Other Essays* (Indianapolis: Hackett, 1991); I. Kant, *Critique of Pure Reason*, ed. and trans. Paul Guyer and Allen Wood (Cambridge: Cambridge University Press, 1998); B. Spinoza, *Ethics*, ed. Matthew J. Kisner, trans. Michael Silverthorne (Cambridge: Cambridge University Press, 2018), pt. 1; W. Rowe, *The Cosmological Argument* (Princeton: Princeton University Press, 1975); R. Koons, "A New Look at the Cosmological Argument," *American Philosophical Quarterly* 34 (1997): 193-212; A. Pruss, *The Principle of Sufficient Reason* (New York: Cambridge University Press, 2006); and R. Byerly, "From a Necessary Being to a Perfect Being," *Analysis* 79 (2019): 10-17.

nothing is both true and not true. The rules of logic constitute the core of reason and underwrite all mathematics and science. I will use logic, then, to underwrite the basic structure of my bridge.

With rules of logic in hand, I will first hammer down steps that provide the floor of the bridge. These steps are certain propositions about reality. I will begin by pinning down several propositions about reality as a whole. In particular, I will show that nothing serves as an outside cause or outside explanation of reality as a whole. In this sense, reality—taken as a whole—is *self-sufficient*. I will then systematically draw out the implications of self-sufficiency. Each implication is a step along the bridge toward a greater understanding of an ultimate foundation of reality. Toward the end of my construction, I will install an archway of lights to highlight a most basic and special feature of this foundation. The completed bridge leads to a grand theory, perhaps the grandest conceivable theory, about ultimate reality.

After the bridge is complete, I will test its integrity by examining obstacles to the grand theory. These obstacles are negative features within the world. The negative features inspire lurking questions about how the foundation could fit with the effects we see. My task will be to provide some tools to help us separate the clear from the unclear. If successful, we will have an open path to a great treasure revealed by reason.

THE FIRST STEP

Let us begin constructing the bridge. To get started, we need *something*. More specifically, we need the premise that there *is* something.

Suppose, instead, there were nothing. In that case, *you* would not be reading this book. For if there were nothing, then there would be no you. Furthermore, the entire enterprise of seeking after truth would be completely pointless—for there would be no truth. There wouldn't even be any books.

Yet you are reading this book. Therefore, there is not merely nothing.

You might wonder whether everything could be a mere dream or an illusion. Still, *even if* everything is a dream, the dream itself exists. If everything is an illusion, the experience of your illusion exists. Besides, there is you—the one to whom things seem a certain way. You cannot begin to be deceived if there is *no one* to be deceived. If you doubt that anything exists, then *doubt* exists. Doubt is something. Therefore, something exists.

When I say something exists, I do not mean anything technical. Ordinary examples illustrate the meaning. Rocks exist. People exist. Atoms exist. Your thoughts exist. This book exists. And so on.

If you press me for a definition, I will say this: "X exists" = "There is such a thing as X."[2] For example, there is such a thing as this coffee mug next to me. It exists.

The above definition exchanges the term *exists* for the phrase "there is such a thing as." You might wonder: What does that phrase mean? If you press me for a further definition, I will say this: "There is such a thing as X" = "X is a member of some category." For example, my coffee mug is a member of the category "mug," among other categories. In general, a thing exists if it is a member of at least some category.

I make no claim about which categories have members. Maybe there are no mugs. Perhaps, instead, I see a hologram of a mug. Then "hologram" is a category, and this mug-like image is a member.

We could keep going on with further definitions. You could now ask what I mean by "member of a category." Of the writing of definitions, there is no end. Yet definition must stop somewhere.

I trust I have said enough to convey the basic idea. The idea is that existing things include all things, whatever their nature. I make no claim about *which* things in particular exist. All we need is *something*, whatever it might be.

The observation that something exists may seem trivial. However, it has profound implications, as we shall see.

THE BLOB OF EVERYTHING

We will begin to see a puzzling implication of existence as we zoom out to consider *all of existence*. To prepare us for the puzzle, I will next hammer down three basic principles about reality as a whole. These principles compose our next step. I will use the instrument of reason.

---

[2]This definition follows the method for talking about what exists in W. V. O. Quine, "On What There Is," *The Review of Metaphysics* 2, no. 5 (1948): 21-38; "Quantifiers and Propositional Attitudes," *The Journal of Philosophy* 53, no. 5 (1956): 177-87; Cf. P. Van Inwagen, "Meta-Ontology," *Erkenntnis* 48, nos. 2-3 (1998): 233-50.

Once this step is in place, we will be ready to see a startling puzzle about existence.

To help us think about reality in total, we can think of all that exists as a big *blob*. This blob includes all particles, all people, all planets, and everything else. It even includes abstract ideas, like numbers, if there are any. As long as something exists (step one), then there is all of it. We can then define "blob of everything" as referring to all that exists.

I make no assumptions at the outset about which sorts of things the blob of everything includes. If there *are* numbers, unicorns, or invisible flying spaghetti monsters (for more on this last example, see venganza.org), then the blob of everything includes them. I leave open how big it is, how old it is, what it is composed of, and so on. I say here just that the blob of everything, by definition, includes all that exists, whatever exists.

Going Deeper

Some philosophers have proposed that no single thing includes all things. Instead, the universe is a plurality of many small things.[3] The small things do not compose a single Big Thing. Rather, our universe is just many things arranged in a certain way. Just as a flock of birds is not a single thing, so too our universe is not a single thing. The term *universe* refers to things.

Fortunately, we don't need to pick a fight with these philosophers. Maybe they are right. Then we could say the "totality" is nothing more than many individual things. In that case, "the blob of everything" refers to the plurality of all things rather than to a single Big Thing. While this distinction between many things vs. one Big Thing is interesting, it makes no difference to the construction of my bridge. Whether the blob of everything is singular or plural, the blob of everything includes all reality.

---

[3]T. Merricks, *Objects and Persons* (Oxford: Oxford University Press, 2001), for example, argues that only *organisms* have parts. See also P. van Inwagen, *Material Beings* (Ithaca, NY: Cornell University Press, 1990).

We are ready to hammer down our first principle about reality as a whole:

Principle 1. No existing thing is outside (i.e., not included among) the blob of everything.

This principle is deducible from our definition. The blob of everything, by definition, includes all existing things. Therefore, whatever is *not* included in the blob of everything does not exist.

From this first principle, we can deduce a second principle:

Principle 2. Nothing outside the blob of everything *caused* the blob of everything to exist.

This principle is deducible from the first. We can display the deduction as follows:

1. The blob of everything includes all that exists (by definition).
2. Therefore, no existing thing is outside the blob of everything (Principle 1).
3. Therefore, no existing *cause* is outside the blob of everything.
4. Therefore, no existing cause outside the blob of everything caused the blob of everything to exist (Principle 2).

In short, nothing is outside the blob of everything, and therefore nothing outside the blob caused the blob.

This result has the power to remove at least one significant theory of everything. I have heard it proposed that Something—or *Someone*—is the transcendent cause of everything. But that cannot be true. Principle 2 contradicts a strict interpretation of the proposal. For if Something transcends all things, then this Something is not among the existing things. In that case, there is a Something that is not something—and we have a contradiction.

To avoid the contradiction, we should distinguish between something that transcends *all* and something that transcends all *else*. Nothing can transcend all. Nothing is beyond all. Therefore, nothing outside existence caused existence. This result is significant, and I will seek to tease out its implications.

Going Deeper

How does time play in? Could an earlier state of the universe cause the current blob of everything? If so, then Principle 2 is false: something "outside" the current blob of everything is its cause. I must clarify, then, that the blob of everything does not merely include all of current reality. It includes all things at all times. For example, suppose a spatial-temporal universe exists. Then the blob of everything includes every temporal slice in the spatial-temporal universe. When I say that the blob of everything has no outside cause, I mean that there is never anything, or any things, beyond the blob of everything (time inclusive).

This result is independent of theories of time. On some theories, the past is not real, while on others, the past is as real as the present. If the past is not real, then the past cannot be a real cause of all reality. If, on the other hand, the past is real, then all reality includes the past. Either way, nothing real is outside all reality.

The third and final principle is like the second:

Principle 3. Nothing outside the blob of everything *explains* why or how the blob of everything exists.

Just as nothing outside the blob of everything caused the blob of everything to exist, so too nothing outside the blob of everything could serve as its ultimate explanation. Unlike a house that stands on the earth, existence in total stands on nothing. Nothing "under" or "beyond" the blob of everything provides a foundation or explanation for the existence of the blob of everything.

Again, to be very clear, nothing is beyond the blob of everything. Hence, nothing beyond the blob of everything could provide an explanation of its existence. Nothing outside existence explains existence.

We are now an inch away from something extremely strange. Before we look closer at the strangeness of existence, I want to say a few things about the tool of reason we are using.

THE POWER OF REASON

You might worry that grand questions about ultimate realty are *too grand* for anyone to answer. Just as a grasshopper cannot fathom the nature of a tree, we cannot hope to fathom the nature of ultimate reality. This worry invites intellectual humility.

While humility will serve us, I want to draw attention to some special and rarely recognized powers of reason. The initial principles about the blob of everything illustrate that reason has at least some power to reveal some far-reaching things. Reason is a light that shines far beyond our local planet. Perhaps you have no idea what exists beyond the Andromeda galaxy. Yet, reason reveals *something*: with reason in hand, you can "see" that there are no square circles floating in deep space.

Logic is like a telescope that lets you see something about *everything*, everywhere. For example, you can see that no contradictions exist on any planet. No matter how far you travel, you will never find a place where something is both *true* and *not true*. You might find a green alien. But you will never find a green alien that is simultaneously *not* green at all. From earth, then, you can see that all regions of space are free from square circles, forceless forces, and colorless green aliens.

Reason has another special power. Reason not only has the power to reveal something about everything, it also has the power to reveal some things crystal *clearly*. Consider, for example, the hypothesis that no square circles exist on Jupiter. You can see the truth of this hypothesis clearly by the light of reason. You do not need to check the soil on Jupiter or trust anyone's report. Rather, the light of reason gives you a way to see with crystal clarity that Jupiter's soil has no square circles buried underneath. There is no *chance* of that.

I am not saying we cannot make mistakes in reasoning. Obviously we can. Mistakes are common. We can misuse reason. With reason in hand, we risk "rationalizing" falsehoods.

In my experience, the key to minimizing error is intellectual humility. When we misuse reason, some part of us knows things aren't *perfectly* clear. The problem is not with reason per se but with how we use it. Instead of using reason to "rationalize" a worldview, we can use reason to aim for truth.

We can also minimize error by combining reason with other evidences. For example, with reason, we can test a theory's logical consistency and then draw out implications. We can go on to test the implications by making further observations. In this way, we can combine reason with experience to make our path to truth more secure.

As we continue on our journey, I will seek to use reason to separate the *clear* from the *unclear*. Some things are unclear. For example, empirical science sometimes exposes paradoxes, like when light behaves as a wave and as a particle, or when quantum particles appear to lack a definitive location. It may be unclear how to make sense of these observations. But even while some things are unclear, other things can be clear by the light of reason.

The unclear sometimes gets in the way of the clear. For example, when scientific experiments indicate that space *curves* or that light behaves like a wave and a particle, these results can inspire doubts about the reliability of reason itself. How can we trust our reason if it contradicts our observations?

However, we can separate observations that are paradoxical from observations that contradict reason. It may be paradoxical *how* space could curve, but it is not contradictory. A paradox is something we *do not see* how to put together, whereas a contradiction is something we *do see* cannot go together.

While the results of science can indeed challenge our intuitions, true science cannot contradict true logic. Logic is foundational to science itself. Without logic, you could never distinguish a theory T from *not* T. Similarly, you could never distinguish evidence for T from evidence for *not* T. Without logic, you could never be sure that any *true* theory is not also *false*. The distinction between true and false collapses without logic. Without logic, science has no power. With logic, we have a foundation for seeing many things.

In general, the more you use a tool, the better you get at using it. The more you use a musical instrument, for example, the better you get at playing that instrument. The more you use your ears to listen, the more sounds you notice. The more you use the tool of reason, the more you can see with it.

Logic can help us see some things clearly. We can see, for example, that a square is not a circle. If we say at the outset that reason *cannot* reveal anything about ultimate reality, then we have already said something about ultimate reality—i.e., that it is unknowable by reason. How could we know that? While it is right to be humble, the hypothesis that reason cannot shine light on grand truths is *itself* a grand hypothesis.

When I first began working with reason, I vastly underestimated its powers. I did not realize it could bring light to so many things. I did not understand the nature of reason. That understanding came later, as I will share in chapter ten, "Foundation of Reason."

As I continue to build the bridge, I will use reason, then, to seek clear lines. I will test coherence and investigate predictions. I will consider relevant observations that will help us test whether the predictions match actual reality. My aim is to use reason to secure a path to truth.

A STRANGE PUZZLE ABOUT EXISTENCE

We have begun our journey by hammering down some basic principles about reality. On one level, these principles may seem trivial. After all, who can deny that something exists, or that nothing is outside everything?

However, let us not mistake the *clear* for the *trivial*. Reason makes it clear that nothing exists beyond all that exists. This result is far from trivial, however. It implies that the blob of everything has the following strange feature: *the blob of everything has no outside explanation or outside cause of its existence.*

This feature is strange because the things we observe in ordinary experience have outside explanations and causes. The chair I am sitting on, for example, did not just snap into existence from nowhere. Something produced it.

Even complex systems, like computers, solar systems, and galaxies, emerge from prior states of reality. Indeed, every chunk of reality—big or small—appears to depend upon other things. If you can think of exceptions, surely they are not part of our everyday experience. Exceptions are odd, unusual, and strange.

Yet the blob of everything is an exception.

Something is deeply puzzling here. How can something exist without any outside cause or explanation? Things we normally experience in life have an explanation *beyond* themselves. Again, my chair exists. Prior causal factors explain its existence. The explanation of my chair is not wholly *within* my chair. The agents that produced the chair are not part of the chair. Those agents transcend the chair. All objects we experience are like this: they have an explanation for their existence, and that explanation transcends their existence. How, then, can reality *in total* lack an outside explanation?

Now one might initially think the answer is simply this: the totality lacks an outside explanation precisely because it is the *totality*. After all, it is not possible that a totality has an outside explanation. It has no explanation beyond itself simply because it *cannot* have an explanation beyond itself.

This answer, however, leaves open a more basic question about *how* any totality can exist without an outside explanation. How is it possible for a reality of any size or shape to exist without any outside explanation?

Think about it this way. Suppose the blob of everything includes some *basic* elements, like particles, that exist without an outside cause or explanation. These elements are then special things unlike all other things we experience. How can there be things like that? What makes them able to be different from everything else?

Or suppose instead that the blob of everything includes only things that have an outside explanation, things like chairs, planets, and galaxies. But then it is puzzling how the things that have an outside explanation could add up to something that does not. How is that even possible?

To see the puzzle from another direction, consider a small blob of Play-Doh. This blob has a *dependent nature*: its existence depends on prior causes, such as a factory that produced it. Now imagine subtracting everything else from existence besides this Play-Doh. Then the Play-Doh exists alone. It now occupies *all* of reality. But that contradicts the nature of the Play-Doh. The Play-Doh has a dependent nature, and we didn't imagine any change to its nature. The problem is that the Play-Doh is the wrong *sort of thing* to occupy all of reality. It is the wrong sort of thing to be able to exist without an outside explanation. But then, what could?

While we can imagine a blob of Play-Doh occupying all of reality, this imagination doesn't reveal *how* this blob could exist. How can any blob of any size (finite or infinite) exist without an outside explanation? To answer this question, we will need to look deeper.

SUMMARY

This chapter introduces the bridge of reason. To take the first step onto the bridge, see that *something exists*. It can be anything: you, your thoughts, or your doubts. If you agree that something exists, then you have taken the first step onto the bridge.

The next step is to see a puzzle. The puzzle is about existence in total. By reason, we can see that nothing exists outside all of existence. It follows, by reason, that our total reality has no cause or explanation outside it. This result is puzzling: how can any reality—of any size—lack an outside cause or outside explanation?

CHAPTER 3

THE FOUNDATION THEORY

In the previous chapter, we stumbled upon a strange puzzle. The purpose of this chapter is to provide a solution to that puzzle.

Consider the puzzle again. We observe, by reason, that the reality as a whole—the *blob of everything*—includes everything. Therefore, nothing exists *beyond* the total blob, and nothing beyond the blob of everything could have caused or explained its existence. In this sense, our reality is "self-sufficient" (i.e., it has no outside cause or explanation). That is strange. How can *anything*—of any size, shape, or number—be self-sufficient?

At this point, we need to start building supports for our bridge of reason. I will install three support beams that provide a foundation for solving the puzzle of existence. These beams will also provide a foundation for our entire pathway to come.

Here, briefly, is the schematic of the solution I will develop: the world includes a *foundation*—a ground layer. The foundation of existence is like the foundation of a bridge. Just as a bridge cannot stand without a foundation, similarly, reality as a whole cannot "stand" in existence without some foundation that stands on its own.

The foundational layer, in other words, provides the ultimate basis for the existence of everything else. The foundation of things enables there to *be* things as opposed to there being nothing at all. Call this account of existence "the Foundation Theory."

The Foundation Theory requires development. How does a foundation *itself* exist? If we say that reality is "self-sufficient" in virtue of having a self-sufficient foundation, we have pushed back the mystery. How does a *foundation* manage to be self-sufficient? What explains the foundation? If nothing, how is that possible?

These questions are among the most fundamental and powerful questions anyone can ask. By thinking carefully about them, we will gain resources for our journey. By putting light on the foundation of things, we also put light on *everything else*. As Harvard philosopher Robert Nozick puts it, "To see how, in principle, a whole realm could fundamentally be explained greatly increases our understanding of the realm."[1] By increasing our understanding of the foundation of everything, we can increase our understanding of everything.

Let us have a closer look at the foundation, then. Let us see what we can see.

FIRST BEAM: INDEPENDENCE

The whole of reality is self-sufficient (with nothing outside to cause or explain its existence). *How*? If self-sufficiency is a locked door, the key to unlock it is this: *independence*. Here is what I mean: in order for any realm of any size to be self-sufficient, that realm must contain some *independent* layer or component. I will explain how this principle works and why I think it is true using three layers of thought.

Layer 1: Root of self-sufficiency. The first thought is about the remarkable difference between a *self-sufficient* realm and a *dependent* realm. The blob of everything has no outside cause or outside explanation, since it includes everything. Your sock drawer, by contrast, is not like that: something beyond the drawer made the drawer and your socks inside.

What accounts for this difference between self-sufficient realms and a realm that is not self-sufficient? What makes the difference between the explained and the unexplained, the caused and the uncaused, the dependent and the independent? What is the *root* of self-sufficiency?

Here is the beginning of an answer: we can account for the difference between your socks (which have an outside explanation) and the blob of everything (which has no outside explanation) in terms of *independence*. The blob of everything includes something that has an

[1]R. Nozick, *Anarchy, State, and Utopia* (New York: Basic Books, 1974), 8.

independent nature. This independent nature is the engine of existence that enables the totality to exist.

Your socks, by contrast, only exist because something produced them. They have a *dependent* nature. For this reason, your socks cannot be the foundation of all existence.

Let us look more closely at the difference between dependence and independence. Logic divides all conceivable realities into two categories: (1) dependent upon another, and (2) *not* dependent upon another. The first—*dependent upon another*—includes anything (like socks) that depends upon some reality beyond itself. In the second category, we have independent things: things that *do not depend upon anything beyond themselves*.

Going Deeper

What about *self-dependence*? I include self-dependence under independence. What matters for our purposes is that the foundation does not depend on something beyond itself. Whether the foundation depends on itself or fails to depend on anything is debatable yet irrelevant. For the sake of focus, then, I will treat self-dependence and non-dependence under a single umbrella, which I'll call *independence*. An independent thing does not depend upon anything beyond itself.

We are now in position to dig to the root of self-sufficiency. The root is *independence*. From independence flows two types of self-sufficient things. One way to be self-sufficient is to *be* an independent thing (or collective). The other way to be self-sufficient is to *include* something that has an independent nature.

To illustrate, imagine that some basic, independent elements are themselves self-sufficient. These elements have an independent nature, which means they exist without any outside cause or explanation. They do not inherit their self-sufficiency from anything. They are simply self-sufficient *in themselves*. These self-sufficient elements, then, provide the ultimate *foundation* for everything else.

The blob of everything then inherits its self-sufficiency from these basic elements. The elements also explain why the blob of everything lacks an outside explanation. The blob of everything lacks an outside explanation because it has an independent foundation that lacks an outside explanation by its nature.

We now have a deeper solution to our puzzle. The puzzle was about how there could be a self-sufficient world—a world with no outside cause or outside explanation. We have a key: *independence*.

The picture is this. The independent foundation is self-sufficient in a basic way; it has an *independent nature*. With the foundation in place, the whole world, with everything in it, inherits its self-sufficiency from its foundation. In other words, the self-sufficiency of the world flows from the independence of the foundation.

We can translate this picture into an argument for the existence of an independent layer—that is, a *foundation*—of reality:

1. A realm cannot be self-sufficient without any independent layer (because independence is the root of self-sufficiency).
2. The blob of everything is a self-sufficient realm (because there is nothing beyond everything).
3. Therefore, the blob of everything has an independent foundation.

I have only begun to put the pieces in place. We will next consider why purely dependent layers cannot *by themselves* add up to an independent realm.

Layer 2: Construction. We can gain a deeper insight into how (not) to build a blob of everything by using a principle of construction. The principle is this: purely dependent things by themselves cannot construct a self-sufficient totality. That's because constructing a self-sufficient totality from purely dependent (non–self-sufficient) materials commits a *construction error*. Let me explain.

I begin with a more general observation: while certain constructions are possible, others are impossible. To illustrate a *possible* construction, imagine you have some white marble blocks. You put these blocks together to construct a floor. Then this floor, which consists entirely of white marble blocks, will *itself* be white and marble. We see here that constructing a white floor out of white tiles is possible. But now consider an impossible construction: you can't construct a *non-white* floor from purely *white* tiles. To construct a non-white floor from white tiles commits a construction error. It's not possible.

We can understand the construction error in terms of part-to-whole inheritance, where the wholes in question exist because their parts have certain positions or properties. In the case of the marble floor, the floor *inherits* some properties from its parts. From white tiles, you get a white floor. There are other properties like this. For example, if every tile of the floor has mass, then so does the whole floor. Similarly, if the parts are shiny like glass, so is the whole. In all these cases, the whole inherits the respective property from its parts. Let us call such properties "whole-inherited."

We can see that whole-inherited properties place constraints on construction. For example, since whiteness is whole-inherited, a floor constructed from purely white tiles cannot be *purple*. To construct a purple floor from purely white tiles contradicts the whole-inheritance of whiteness. Therefore, the nature of whiteness constrains the possibilities regarding what you can construct with white tiles.

Notice that the number of tiles is not relevant to whole-inheritance. Whether the floor is made of one tile or infinitely many makes no difference. Even a floor with *infinitely* many white tiles is still white. The constraint on construction comes from the nature of the tiles, not their number.

The constraints on construction point us again to the need for a foundation. Without a foundation, every layer of reality is *dependent*. Yet dependent layers—of any size and number—are insufficient for constructing an independent blob of everything. Just as white tiles yield a white floor, dependent parts yield a dependent whole.

Examples illustrate the principle. Suppose you have two tiles. Each tile has a dependent nature: these tiles do not exist on their own. Now suppose you put those tiles together to form a small floor. Then this floor is also dependent. From dependent parts, you form a dependent floor. In particular, the causes of the tiles, together with your work to put the tiles together, provide the basis for the resulting floor. The floor, then, is also dependent, just like the tiles that compose it.

In general, adding dependent things together results in a dependent total. Increasing the number of things makes no difference. We will not transform a floor into a non-dependent, self-sufficient totality just by adding more and more dependent tiles together.

Increasing the age also makes no difference. Imagine a floor has existed for a year. This floor is not thereby *independent*. A floor composed of dependent tiles is a dependent floor *for as long as it exists*. Even if a floor exists for infinitely many years, the floor depends on its tiles for as long as they exist. To form a non-dependent (self-sufficient) floor from purely dependent tiles, of any age, commits a construction error.

Let us give this principle about dependence a name:

Dependence Principle: purely dependent things form dependent totals.

This principle—that purely dependent things form dependent totals—not only matches experience, it also matches reason. It is like the principle that a floor composed of purely white tiles is a white floor. By understanding the concepts in this principle, you can sense, via reason, a connection between purely white tiles and the whiteness of the total floor. In the same way, I propose for your consideration that you can sense a connection between purely *dependent* tiles and the dependence of a total floor. Just as white tiles compose a white floor, dependent tiles compose a dependent floor.

Let us take a step back to see where we are. Here is the picture. The blob of everything exists. Yet it has no outside cause or outside explanation. How is that? The foundation explains how. A foundation supplies an *independent nature* at the floor of reality. Without an independent nature, by contrast, we have the construction problem. For then everything has a purely dependent nature, yet *dependence* is an insufficient basis for a blob that is *not* dependent. To avoid the construction error, then, we need a non-dependent foundation.[2]

Layer 3: Inheritance (extra). I want to go deeper, if I can. I will offer you something I have not seen in any book or article on this subject. This third layer includes an idea I have about whole-inheritance (as I will explain). If the idea is right, it can help us see an even deeper reason why dependent things cannot be the ultimate building blocks of our world.

---

[2]The picture leaves open what philosophers call "priority monism," where reality as a *whole* is the independent foundation. See J. Schaffer, "Monism," *Stanford Encyclopedia of Philosophy* (2018), https://plato.stanford.edu/entries/monism/.

(If you are ready to look into the nature of an independent foundation, feel free to skip ahead.)

To get started, consider again some examples of "whole-inherited" properties: whiteness, mass, and glassiness. Each of these properties is "diffusive." Here is what I mean. A diffusive property spans arbitrary subsections. For example, a marble block is marble throughout its subsections. That is why if you break a marble tile into pieces, each piece will also be marble. The marble "diffuses" throughout the marble tile. Whiteness is the same way. It spans a white surface: every section of a white piece of paper is also white. The same goes for mass: arbitrary sections of a massive tile also have mass. Sections of a glassy floor are also glassy. And so on.

Consider, by contrast, properties that are *not* diffusive. Take triangularity. A triangular tile is not triangular in arbitrary subsections. If you shatter a triangular tile, there is a good chance *none* of the pieces will be precisely triangular. That is because triangularity does not diffuse down into arbitrary subsections. Non-diffusive properties do not span arbitrary subsections, whereas diffusive properties do.

Two clarifications are in order. First, a diffusive property diffuses in things of any size or shape. For example, marble diffuses in a large castle or a small chess piece. By contrast, *being smaller than Earth* doesn't diffuse into anything bigger than Earth. So it doesn't count as diffusive. A diffusive property, to be precise, includes no region-restricting information, like a quantity or comparison. We could say diffusive properties—like marble, whiteness, glass, and so on—are purely *qualitative*, not *quantitative*.

Second, we need not be concerned with diffusing down into arbitrarily small magnitudes. For example, glass is ultimately divisible into atoms, yet no atom is glassy. In that sense, glassiness is not *purely* diffusive. Nevertheless, beyond some minimal scale, the "glassiness" spans arbitrary subsections: the top half, bottom quarter, right corner, etc., are all glassy.

Now you may have been wondering, what makes a property *whole-inherited*? For example, what makes whiteness whole-inherited but not triangularity? I have a proposal for you:

Principle of Inheritance: whatever is diffusive is whole-inherited.

To illustrate, consider again the white marble tiles. Both the whiteness and the marble quality of the tiles span arbitrary subsections of each tile. In other words, both whiteness and marble are diffusive. According to the Principle of Inheritance, then, whiteness and marble are also whole-inherited. It follows that a floor composed of white marble tiles is both white and marble—just as we would expect.

I offer the Principle of Inheritance as a working hypothesis. My reason to think this hypothesis can help guide us is that it makes correct predictions. Marble, whiteness, mass, and glassiness are all diffusive, and, just as predicted, they are all whole-inherited. Here is a longer catalog of diffusive properties: colors, textures, densities, and being homogenous. The Principle of Inheritance predicts correct results for each of these. Good news. I invite you to test out additional examples to investigate the principle further for yourself. My proposal is that the principle is at least a good guide.[3]

Reason itself provides a second witness to the Principle of Inheritance. In particular, by reason one can see a connection between diffusive and whole-inherited. Diffusive properties span arbitrary subsections: for example, a glass tile is glassy in arbitrary sections. For this reason, if you break the marble tile, its pieces will all be marble. Now suppose after breaking the tile, you put these arbitrary pieces together again. You can put them together in any way you wish. Since the marble pieces are arbitrary pieces, you could put them together in any arbitrary way, and the result is still marble. Arbitrary recombination is key. By arbitrary recombination, the properties that span *inward* to their parts (i.e., they are diffusive) thereby span *outward* to the whole (i.e., they are whole-inherited). Thus, diffusive properties are whole-inherited.

Suppose the Principle of Inheritance is indeed a good guide. We can then use the Principle of Inheritance to probe reality as a whole. In particular, the Principle of Inheritance gives us another way to see a non-dependent

[3]Graham Oppy asked me in a personal correspondence about the property of *reflecting light*. This property is diffusive, yet it is not whole-inherited, he suggested, because matter does not reflect light if it has enough mass to collapse into a black hole. This example serves to clarify the concept of inheritance. I do not claim that inherited properties apply to wholes under *any* condition. They only apply to wholes when they also apply to their parts. In the case of black holes, *none of the parts reflect light*. So this case is not a counterexample.

layer, that is, a foundation. Here is how. Either dependence is diffusive or not. Consider first the option that dependence is diffusive. Then, by the Principle of Inheritance, dependence is whole-inherited. In other words, everything formed from dependent things is itself dependent on an outside reality. But, of course, the blob of *everything* is not dependent on any outside reality. It follows, then, the blob of everything is not formed from purely dependent things. It must include a non-dependent layer.

Consider next the option that dependence is not diffusive (or not purely diffusive). Then dependent things are *not* formed entirely from dependent subsections. In other words, at least some dependent things include something *foundational* (non-dependent)—and thus the Foundation Theory follows. So either way (whether dependence is diffusive or not), reality has a non-dependent layer.

We now have in place materials for a deeper understanding of self-sufficiency. Each of the three layers in this first beam of our bridge supports the following result: an independent, self-sufficient foundation exists. From this information, we can understand how a blob—such as a blob of everything—can be self-sufficient. It is self-sufficient because it has a foundation that is self-sufficient *by nature*. Like a bridge that stands by having a foundation, the blob of everything exists by having an ultimate foundation.

SECOND BEAM: NECESSITY

We do not yet have a complete solution to the puzzle of existence. If we say that the world exists because its foundation exists, we can still ask how its foundation exists. How can anything be a *foundation*?

The question at hand is about the difference between a foundational thing and non-foundational, dependent things. What could explain the difference? Suppose there are two beings: Rob and Bob. Let's say Rob depends for his existence on something, whereas Bob does not depend on anything. What could explain the difference between Rob and Bob? What is it about *Rob* that makes him dependent, while *Bob* is not?

Here are some answers that don't seem to work. First, mere differences in *shape* don't explain the difference. Imagine Rob has the shape of a triangle, while Bob has the shape of a square. These differences do not explain how Rob is dependent, while Bob is not. What does shape have to do with dependence? Nothing.

Size is equally irrelevant. Say Bob is one thousand times bigger than Rob. Will Bob's great size explain how Bob can exist without a source? Clearly not.

How, then, can Bob exist without a source? How can it be independent? If we answer that Bob is independent by containing some non-dependent, fundamental parts, we still have not explained how Bob's fundamental parts can be independent. The question remains: how can *anything* be independent?

While this question is deep, I believe it is answerable. From the time of Aristotle, philosophers have uncovered the materials for an account of an independent nature. Let us have a look at their answers.[4]

Here is the account: the difference between a dependent Rob and an independent, self-sufficient Bob arises ultimately from a difference in the nature of the parts that make up Rob and Bob. More specifically, Bob contains some fundamental parts that have a *necessary nature.*

To unpack the concept of a "necessary nature," suppose you have some clay in your hand. This clay, let us say, can be formed into many different shapes. For example, you could mold the clay into the shape of a mug. Suppose you do just that: you form a mug out of the clay. Then the mug you form exists. But nothing *requires* that this mug exist. You could smash it as easily as you formed it. Thus, the mug does not have a necessary nature.

Consider what it means to lack a necessary nature. To say that the mug lacks a necessary nature is to say it *could be gone*. When I say it could be gone, I mean that the mug could fail to exist at some time. In other words, there can be some time at which that mug does not actually exist.

Something with a necessary nature is different. Suppose the *clay* (but not the mug) has no potential not to exist. Its nature, then, is necessary. This clay is very special clay because its non-existence at any time is simply impossible. If there were clay like this, it would be

---

[4]See Aristotle, *Metaphysics*, trans. Joe Sachs (New Mexico: Green Lion Press, 2002), book 7 for the seed form. See also R. Koons, "A New Look at the Cosmological Argument," *American Philosophical Quarterly* 34 (1997): 193-212.

impossible for anything to bring it into existence or to take it out of existence. Such clay would have permanent existence because it would have *necessary existence*.

I have been seeking to explain the difference between necessary existence and non-necessary existence. The ancient Greek philosopher Aristotle explains this difference in terms of *potentiality*. Before you formed the mug, it was merely a *potential* reality. In order for that potential reality to become actual, something had to make it *actual*. The hypothetical clay, by contrast, is necessarily actual (we are assuming). Therefore, it never passes from a merely potential reality into an actual reality. Nothing could actualize it, since it is necessarily "already" actual.

To clarify these ideas further, I will express them from a contemporary angle. Philosophers these days talk about "possible worlds."[5] While there are different theories about the nature of a possible world, the basic concept of a possible world is this: a possible world is a complete way reality might *possibly* have been. For example, if there could have been fewer quarks, then there is a possible world according to which there are fewer quarks.

We can display the difference between a non-necessary thing and a necessary thing using the language of possible worlds. A non-necessary thing, like a mug, exists in some but *not* all possible worlds. A necessary thing, by contrast, exists in all possible worlds. To be clear, if the world has *times*, the necessary thing exists simpliciter regardless of the time. (I will say more about the relationship between a necessary thing and time in chapter five, "Eternal Power.")

With these clarifications in mind, we are ready to return to our question: how can the foundation have an independent nature? Here is my answer: the foundation can have an independent nature by having a *necessary* nature. By the necessity of its existence, the foundation is able to be a foundation. From necessity springs independence.

Necessity makes sense of independence. We can think of the foundation as a platform. Suppose this platform has necessary existence. Then nothing exists *prior to* the platform. The platform already exists prior to all else. Hence, nothing prior to the platform could provide an

---

[5]See A. Plantinga, *Nature of Necessity* (New York: Oxford University Press, 1974), 44.

outside cause or explanation of its existence. In other words, the platform couldn't depend on any prior cause or explanation. A necessary platform is *automatically actual*, without any prior cause or explanation.

Going Deeper

You may wonder whether some necessary things could still depend on other necessary things. Consider, for example, the number 1 and the set {1}. You might think the number 1 exists "prior to" {1}, even though neither can exist without the other. In this way, you could imagine necessary realities having multiple layers, with some layers being prior to others. Call this sense of priority, *priority of nature*.

To be clear, then, the notion of "prior" I am working with is different. When I say "prior condition," I mean a condition that is prior in existence. For example, the clay is prior to the mug's existence in the sense that the clay can exist without the mug. We might think of this priority as a priority of substance rather than a mere *priority of nature*.

In any case, here is the upshot: while we may theorize that the foundation of reality has multiple dependent layers within its nature, still, nothing is prior in substance to the entire foundation as a whole. The necessity of the foundation, then, entails its ability to exist independent from any prior substance.

This difference between necessary existence and non-necessary existence accounts, then, for the difference between a *dependent* being and an *independent* (and self-sufficient) being. We can capture this result with a pair of principles:

Principle of Self-Sufficiency: whatever has a *self-sufficient* nature *has* a necessary nature.

Principle of Insufficiency: whatever has a *dependent* nature *lacks* a necessary nature.

These principles give us a deeper account of the blob of everything. They help us answer this question: how can the blob be self-sufficient? Here is how: there is a ground layer, a foundation, that is self-sufficient *by nature*. How can the foundation be self-sufficient by nature? Here is how: the foundation has a necessary nature; it has no potential not to exist. This foundation, then, has a special nature that explains how it can exist without *depending* on anything.

We now have two beams that support our steps. Both beams independently support the same result: in order for there to be a world, *any* world, there must be an independent foundation underlying everything else.

THIRD BEAM: ULTIMACY

One of the deepest questions anyone can ask is this: why is there anything? We have the power to ask *why* and *how* things exist. For example, when we encounter an object—of any shape or size—we can wonder how that object got there. We may extend such questions to groups of objects. Why are there these kittens under my couch? Why are there planets? Why are there solar systems? Why are there galaxies? It is inevitable that people will wonder about the whole show: *why is there anything*?

In view of the challenge of hard questions like this, some people throw up their hands and say there is no answer. However, if we say there is no answer, then we face the problem of *arbitrary unexplained existence*.

Think of any object, big or small. We can at least conceive of an explanation of its existence: for example, we can conceive of causes that produce it, or we can conceive of an explanation in terms of the Principle of Self-Sufficiency (i.e., it exists because it cannot not exist). But suppose a random turtle happens to have no explanation at all. That would be strange. It would be strange because an unexplained turtle would be unlike everything else we know. Its *lack of explanation* would be arbitrary.

Consider what arbitrary, unexplained existence implies. Suppose some object O exists with no explanation. No cause explains it. No necessary nature explains it. Instead, O just happens to exist, and that's that. Then O has the following features: it is (1) actual, (2) potentially not actual (without a necessary nature), yet (3) unactualized.

It turns out, interestingly, that the Principle of Self-Sufficiency precludes this combination of features. I'll show you why. Recall the principle: whatever has a self-sufficient nature has a necessary nature. It follows (by contraposition) that whatever *lacks* a necessary nature *lacks* a self-sufficient nature. In other words, whatever lacks a necessary nature depends on something. But to lack a necessary nature is to have the real potential not to be actual. Therefore, from here, we may deduce the following principle:

Principle of Actuality: Whatever is actual, but potentially not actual, depends on an actualizer.

In other words, nothing can be (1) actual, (2) potentially not actual, yet (3) unactualized.

I will examine the Principle of Actuality very closely in the next chapter. For now, it suffices to highlight a powerful consequence of this principle. This principle provides a solution to the problem of arbitrary unexplained existence. The solution is simple: nothing has arbitrary unexplained existence.

The foundation exists by having a self-sufficient, necessary nature. Everything "above" the foundation has an explanation in terms of whatever actualized it. So, nothing is arbitrarily unexplained.

Without an ultimate foundation, by contrast, it remains unexplained why there is *anything*. The blob of everything would then be like a chicken that pops into existence from nothing. Or, the blob is like an everlasting chicken that can fail to exist at any moment, yet randomly never does. In either case, it remains unexplained why and how there can (still) be anything.

With a foundation, there are, by contrast, no arbitrarily unexplained things. All existing things can have an explanation. Dependent things, for example, exist because of the things they depend on. Moreover, the independent foundation exists because of its own necessary nature.

Suppose we say instead that some things have an explanation, while other things do not. Then we need some principled way to distinguish between cases. Otherwise, we are like someone who claims that some turtles may have snapped into existence without any explanation. The "uncaused turtle" claim contradicts everything we know, and we have no reason to accept it.

Similarly, without a reason to think certain things, whether turtles or big blobs, exist without any explanation, we have no reason to overthrow the general principle that existing things have an explanation for their existence.

We have an answer, then, to an ultimate question about existence: why is there anything? We can arrive at the answer without arrogance. Yes, humility is a virtue. But humility need not stop us from discovering an answer *if one is available*. We have a solution at hand.

The upshot is that the foundation makes sense of existence. With a foundation, there are then no arbitrarily unexplained things. *Dependent* things exist because of the things they depend on. Meanwhile, the *independent foundation* exists because of its own necessary nature. Everything fits together.

We are working with highly dense material. For this reason, I'd like to spend more time probing the material. I will devote the entire next chapter to further examination and clarification of the concepts in this chapter. I will consider a series of classic and contemporary objections to ideas similar to the ones we have been considering here. I will also install an additional piece that further fills out the foundation of the bridge.

SUMMARY

The basic components of our bridge install the Foundation Theory. The Foundation Theory is what it sounds like: there is a foundation to things. Like a stack of bricks that rests upon the ground, the stack of dependent things rests ultimately upon an independent foundation.

The Foundation Theory makes sense of three things. First, it makes sense of how the totality of everything can lack an outside cause or outside explanation. Reason and experience together testify that totals of dependent things are themselves dependent; from dependence comes only dependence. Purely *dependent* things cannot, then, be the basis for the *self-sufficiency* of the totality of things. Instead, the root of self-sufficiency is an independent nature.

Second, the Foundation Theory makes sense of the difference between *potential* realities and *actual* ones. A potential reality is *actual* only if something *actualizes* it. If, instead, the totality of dependent realities lacks any actualizer, then nothing accounts for its actuality. The entire totality would be a *mere potential*. Nothing, then, would be actual. Something is actual, however. Therefore, there is an actualizer of dependent realities. This actualizer is actual *by nature*, with no potential not to be actual. In other words, it has a necessary nature. This necessary nature accounts for how the foundation can be an independent foundation.

Finally, the Foundation Theory makes sense of how there can be anything at all. With a foundation in place, there is something rather than nothing because the foundation has necessary existence. This foundation, then, provides an ultimate foundation for everything else.

CHAPTER 4

TESTING GROUND

So far, we have put into place a foundation for our bridge. In this chapter, we will further examine this foundational structure. I will use nine *tests* that probe and push upon the foundational materials. These tests come from questions, comments, and objections I have encountered over the last twenty years in journal articles, books, academic halls, and the Internet. Then, toward the end of this chapter, I will install a twenty-first century invention that will provide an additional, independent reinforcement of the entire structure of our bridge.

My aim is to provide a better sense of the integrity and nature of the bridge. Feel free to skip to whatever objections interest you most. If you are ready to explore the next steps on the bridge, flip to the next chapter.

OBJECTION 1: INFINITE REGRESS

Objection. The argument for the Foundation Theory assumes, without justification, that the chain of causes and effects must be *finite*. But suppose, instead, the chain is infinite: each state of the universe is like a domino that was knocked into existence by a prior state. Then each state is actualized (made actual) by another state, and there is no *ultimate* foundation.

Reply. I actually do not assume that the chain of causes must be finite. The "infinite regress" objection, though common, does not actually touch the bridge of reason I have been constructing. The principles in my construction have nothing at all to do with the length of history or the size of reality. Maybe reality is infinitely old. Maybe it is finite. Maybe there is one universe. Maybe there is a multiverse. No matter the size or age, we can ask how any reality—of any length or size—could exist. My argument is that without a foundation, there would be nothing, ever. The foundation is not something that comes *before* the chain of causes. Rather, the foundation is the ultimate *basis* of everything across all time.

To see more clearly how this foundation works, consider the following domino story.

> *You wake up in a strange place. The first thing you notice is a domino fall over. You wonder how that happened. You then see that this flat domino lies at the end of a chain of other flat dominoes. As it turns out, this chain has no beginning. There are now infinitely many dominoes lying along an infinite floor. Each domino has been knocked down by the one next to it. The end.*

In this story, we can explain why each domino lies flat: another domino knocked it over. Yet there remains a deeper question about how these dominoes lie *anywhere.* What holds them up? The story has an answer: the floor. The floor acts as a *foundation* for the locations of the dominoes.

Notice that the floor supports the dominoes *while* they are knocking each other. The floor is not some "first" domino that got the rest of the dominoes started. Rather, the floor supports the dominoes at each moment.

In the same way, a self-sufficient foundation can act as a foundation for the existence of dependent things at every moment. To illustrate, suppose the foundation consists of elementary particles. Then these particles underlie everything else at every moment. Without any foundation, by contrast, *dependent* things, like tables and chairs, would never be able to exist at all.

Here is the crucial point: the *number* of causes, whether finite or infinite, is irrelevant to every single step on our bridge. The first step was about existence. It is irrelevant *how many* things exist. Whether the world has infinitely many or finitely many things, still, *something* exists. That's all we need to step onto the bridge.

The next step was about a puzzle. We used reason to deduce something strange about existence in total: reality as a whole has no outside source (i.e., no outside cause or outside explanation). Again, this deduction has nothing to do with the *number* of things. Whether there are infinitely many things or finitely many, still, the totality of all things has no outside source.

Number also has nothing to do with the problem of construction. We saw that some constructions are impossible no matter how many pieces you use. For example, water will never add up to fire. Similarly, dependent things will never add up to a *non-dependent* (self-sufficient) totality.[1] The nature of dependence precludes non-dependence. The number, or amount, of dependent things makes no difference.

Besides this, the Principle of Actuality doesn't depend on number. Recall the principle: any reality that is actual but *potentially not actual* depends upon an actualizer. This principle applies to realities of any size and length, even infinite realities, if there could be realities that large. Imagine an infinite chain of dominoes. Your imagination doesn't make this chain real: if infinitely many dominoes were to be actual, something must actualize this potential. The point, again, is that the number of dominoes is irrelevant. Number has nothing to do with the dominoes' dependence upon some source; even an infinite chain of dominoes will not be actual without any source.

In fact, an infinite chain would only *reinforce* the need for a foundation. Consider this: a foundation explains how things manage to exist for *so long*. If things have always existed, how did they last that long? Why didn't the basic elements simply vanish like vapor a long time ago? With a foundation, we have a solution: things continue to exist because the foundation of reality is unable not to exist. Extending the age of the world out to infinity doesn't undermine this result. It points to it.

I'll close my thoughts here with an observation about why many people raise the "infinite-regress" objection. My observation is that people sometimes raise this objection in response to arguments that explicitly require a finite history—such as a beginning of the universe. These arguments have something in common with my argument: they are about the ultimate source of reality. It may be tempting, therefore, to associate my argument with these arguments for a finite history.

---

[1]I owe this metaphor to Cameron Bertuzzi (in personal correspondence).

Yet by the light of reason, we can see a distinction between the beams in our bridge and the arguments that require a finite history. The distinction is this: our beams hold independently of the length of history. In fact, if anything, an infinite history would *further highlight* the need for a foundation—to explain how things have lasted so long.

OBJECTION 2: FALLACY OF COMPOSITION

Objection. In academic halls and some corners of the Internet, you might hear this complaint about *cosmological* arguments (i.e., arguments for an ultimate cause). They commit a fallacy of "composition."[2] To illustrate this fallacy, consider the following argument:

1. Each section of the universe has a cause.
2. Therefore, the entire universe has a cause.

The problem here is that this argument is not valid because its conclusion, (2), fails to follow from (1). The underlying problem is that the argument implicitly relies on the following fallacious inference from parts to whole: whatever is true of the parts is true of the whole. It is this inference that tempts people to think that if each *part* of the universe has a cause, then so does the *whole* universe.

Yet, the principle from Parts to Wholes is false. It is false that whatever is true of the parts is automatically also true of the whole. For example, it is true of the atoms in your hand that they are atoms, but it is not also true that your whole hand is an atom. Similarly, the parts of a sandwich are not themselves sandwiches. In general, parts can be *different* from the whole they compose.

For this reason, arguments that rely on the Parts to Wholes principle are fallacious. They commit the fallacy of composition: they assume that the whole has all the same properties as its parts. Therefore, it is a fallacy to assume that the whole of the universe has a cause from the observation that parts of the universe have a cause.

---

[2]See D. Hume, *Dialogues Concerning Natural Religion* (Cambridge: Cambridge University Press, 2007 [originally 1779]), 58-59; F. C. Copleston and B. Russell, "A Debate on the Existence of God," BBC (1948), www.scandalon.co.uk/philosophy/cosmological_radio.htm; P. Edwards, "The Cosmological Argument," in *The Rationalist Annual for the Year*, ed. C. Watts, (London: Pemberton, 1959), 63-77.

Reply. This objection, though instructive, does not actually touch any part of our bridge. I did not take the Parts to Wholes principle in hand when I constructed the beams.

Instead, I used other principles. For example, I used a principle of dependence, according to which *dependence* flows from parts to whole. Although it is fallacious to assume that *all* wholes have *all* the properties of their parts, it is not fallacious to infer that *certain* wholes have *certain* properties of their parts. Some properties are indeed whole-inherited: they flow from parts to whole. For example, whiteness, marble, and glassiness flow from parts to whole. Thus, it is not fallacious to infer that a floor composed of white tiles is itself white or that a stack of marble is itself marble. Similarly, it is not fallacious to infer that dependent things form a dependent totality. These inferences track everything we know in experience.

Moreover, the fallacy of composition actually highlights the *strength* of the beams in our bridge. The fallacy of composition highlights the constraints on construction. Consider the following argument:

1. Each section of reality has an outside cause.
2. Therefore, the entirety of reality has an outside cause.

This argument is worse than fallacious: it is contradictory. For, as we saw in chapter two, no cause can be outside all causes. To construct reality, then, we need an unconstructed *foundation*. Otherwise, we commit a construction error.

OBJECTION 3: VIRTUAL PARTICLES

Objection. The Principle of Actuality is out of step with current science. We have evidence that things can appear without any cause or explanation. For example, physicists tell us that "virtual" particles can randomly appear without any cause at all.

Reply. This objection is valuable because it invites a crucial clarification. When we talk about causes and their effects, we can talk about two types of effects: *demanded* effects and *dependent* effects. While all effects are dependent, not all effects are demanded. For example, virtual particles may not be *demanded* by prior states, but it does not follow that these particles do not *depend* on prior states. Demand is different from dependence.

To illustrate the difference, imagine two gumball machines. One has only red gumballs, while the other has both red and blue gumballs. You first drop a quarter into the machine with only red gumballs, and it predictably spits out a red gumball. This result is demanded by the contents of the machine. The setup provides precisely one possible outcome. You then drop a quarter into the other machine, which has both red and blue gumballs. Now you can't predict the color of the gumball you'll get. It could be either red or blue. The contents of the machine don't demand any one color. More than one outcome is possible. If the machine spits out red, this effect was not *demanded* by the machine. It could have spit out blue instead. In other words, the machines differ with respect to the effects they demand. Still, the machines have this in common: their effects, whether a blue gumball or red, are *dependent* on the machine's operations. After all, if the machine breaks, it will never give you any gumball.

In the same way, when a particle "spontaneously" appears or an atom "spontaneously" decays, perhaps nothing demanded that these precise events would happen. Still, it would be a mistake to infer that the events emerged from *nothing*. That doesn't follow. Instead, the particle might emerge spontaneously from a prior energy state, just as some physicists propose. In that case, the particle still depends upon *something*.

Moreover, the existence of spontaneous—*un-demanded*—particles is precisely what we could expect *given* the construction of our bridge. To see why I say this, recall that one of our support beams is the necessity of the foundation. Now either the foundation *demands* all its effects, or the foundation is capable of having spontaneous effects, like virtual particles. The first option—that a foundation demands all its effects—implies that all its effects exist immediately and necessarily. Picture an eternal star that eternally produces light: the star and its light are both eternal. If the foundation were like an eternal star that demands all its effects, then all its effects would likewise be necessary and eternal. Yet not everything is necessary and eternal. The result, then, is that the foundation does not demand (require or necessitate) all its effects. One option remains: the foundation can produce some effects *spontaneously*.

This result fits well with the Principle of Actuality. The Principle of Actuality says that mere potentials cannot become actual without *something* to actualize them. This principle leaves open *how* an actualizer actualizes its effect: maybe it demands the effect, or maybe instead it provides the conditions for the effect to come about spontaneously. In either case, the principle of cause and effect does not contradict science. On the contrary, the principle of cause and effect is foundational to scientific inquiry.

OBJECTION 4: UNCAUSED EVENTS

Objection. The Principle of Actuality is too hasty: just because we never *see* a potential reality become actual on its own from nothing, it is hasty for us to infer that uncaused events couldn't ever happen. In fact, if there were a *first* event, then no event "before" that event could actualize it. Perhaps the totality appeared in a first event from nothing, with no cause or foundation.

Reply. First, let us take a step back and consider what is at stake. In chapter three, I set up three beams to support our steps. Each beam corresponds to an aspect of the foundation: first, the foundation has an independent nature (to account for the self-sufficiency of the totality); second, the foundation has necessary existence (to account for its own independence); third, the foundation is ultimate (to account for the existence of anything at all). The objection at hand targets only the second beam by challenging the foundation's necessary existence. The objection is this: if the foundation of things *came into existence*, then the foundation lacks a necessary nature.

Let us have a closer look, then, at the second beam. This beam includes a principle—the Principle of Actuality—that is about actualizing potentials. The principle is simple: a potential is actual only if something actualizes it. In other words, no potential becomes actual on its own.

I want to unpack why I think this principle is true. To begin, consider an example of a potential, a new iPhone, say. How might this iPhone become actual? We have three options: (1) the potential makes itself actual; (2) something besides the potential makes it actual; (3) nothing makes the potential actual.

Let us consider each option in turn. Option (1) is that the potential makes *itself* actual. For concreteness, suppose an iPhone 2000 is a potential technology. This potential is not actual, but it could be. Now consider what it would mean for this potential to *make itself* actual. Suppose the iPhone 2000 makes itself actual. Then the iPhone 2000 is either already actual or not. If the iPhone 2000 is *already actual*, then it is "too late" for the iPhone 2000 to make itself actual. It's already actual, after all. If, on the other hand, the iPhone 2000 is not actual, then the iPhone 2000 cannot make anything actual—for whatever is *not* actual has no actual capacities. Only something actual has the capacity to make something actual.

You can test this claim by hopping off a cliff. No fictional characters will come to your rescue. Spiderman will not pull himself out of the land of imagination and leap into actual reality to stop your fall. In precisely the same way, if you want to have an iPhone 2000 in your hand, no potential iPhone 2000 will pull itself out of the land of imagination and leap into your hand. It has no power to do that.

A mere *potential* reality, then, has no *actual* powers. Actual powers belong to actual things. If a mere potential (non-actual) iPhone 2000 did have actual power to make itself actual, then this iPhone 2000 would be actual prior to being actual. In other words, the iPhone 2000 would be actual and not actual—which is a contradiction. Reason refuses this result. Hence, option (1) is impossible.

Option (2) is better. It avoids the contradiction. According to this option, something besides the iPhone 2000 makes the iPhone 2000 actual. For example, a factory assembles the iPhone 2000. Here the factory causes a merely *potential* iPhone 2000 to be an *actual* iPhone 2000. Actuality then flows from *actual* things. No contradiction there.

What about option (3)? Could *nothing* make the iPhone 2000 actual? To illustrate this option, imagine the iPhone 2000 just randomly appears in your hand from nowhere. It's not that it *causes itself* to be actual. Rather, the idea here is that the iPhone 2000 snaps into existence without *any* cause. Can that happen?

Consider this test. Hop off a cliff. What might happen? We already saw that fictional characters lack the power to bring *themselves* out of fiction. But we can see something else. Not only can't these characters make themselves exit fiction, they also don't exit fiction spontaneously uncaused. If you hop off a cliff, Spiderman will not enter reality to save you. Neither will any other superhero. There are infinitely many conceivable fictional superheroes, yet not *one* of them will come out of fiction from nothing. All experience confirms this prediction.

The problem is not that superheroes are conceptually impossible, like a square circle. Superheroes are conceptually *possible*. So, the reason they don't exit fiction is not that they *cannot* exist. It's rather that they cannot exit fiction *uncaused*.

The barrier to existence does not only apply to superheroes, of course. Kermit the Frog never exits fiction, either. Neither does Super Mario or Bugs Bunny. Differences in their shapes and sizes make no difference. It is not any easier for a large superhero to exit fiction than for a small superhero. Similarly, it is no easier for a chalice from a Disney story to snap into your hand than for any imagined iPhone to snap into your hand with no source. Differences in shape and size are completely irrelevant to the ability to appear from nowhere.

Consider again the *first* event. Could some initial state of matter, along with some laws, simply appear from nothing? Maybe if there *were* nothing, then everything and anything would be possible, including the emergence of a random universe. Is that possible?

I used to be unsure about whether a first event—if there were a first event—would require any prior condition for its existence. I considered it an open possibility, even if a minimal possibility, that a first event came from nothing. After all, such an event would be far removed from everyday experience. So how could anyone be sure a first event would be anything like other events?

But later I saw a reason to be skeptical that *any* event could be uncaused. Reason can sometimes reveal things far removed from ordinary experience. For example, reason reveals that colorless aliens cannot be green at *any* time or place. Logic acts like a telescope that can extend our vision into remote times and places.

Eventually, I noticed that some differences are plainly irrelevant to the ability to come from nothing. For example, if a Disney princess is unable to appear in front of you from nowhere in the next minute, then neither can *two* Disney princesses. The difference in number is irrelevant to the ability to appear from nowhere. Seeing this irrelevance is like seeing that none of the prime numbers can be a prime minister. You can see plainly that higher numbers are not more capable of being a prime minister than lower numbers. For you can see plainly that differences in number are *irrelevant* with respect to the ability to be a prime minister. In precisely the same way, it is possible to see that differences in number are irrelevant with respect to the ability to appear from nothing: if one princess can appear from nowhere, then so can two.

In the same way, differences in size, shape, and spatiotemporal location are irrelevant differences. If, for example, an actual chicken has no way of coming into being from nowhere on top of your lap today, then a chicken cannot come into being from nowhere on your lap tomorrow.

The same is so for a special object with its own special laws. If an object—with its own laws—cannot appear from nowhere at one place and time, it cannot appear from nowhere at any other place or time.

Again, size doesn't matter: an object could be the size of a pea, or it could be the size of a galaxy, or bigger still. Just as bigger prime numbers are not more or less able to be prime ministers, so too, bigger objects are not more or less able to appear from nowhere. If you jump off a cliff, it will not be easier for a *big* Superman to leave the land of fiction and rescue you than for a micro Superman to do that. Differences in size have nothing to do with the ability of a potential to be actual uncaused.

Does it matter what an object *contains*? Plainly not. A Disney princess that contains a tiny universe inside her heart will not have an easier time appearing from nowhere in front of you this afternoon than any other Disney princess. Similarly, it is no easier for some blob to appear from nowhere if the blob includes all people than if it includes all particles. The contents are irrelevant.

Consider again the first event. This event—if there is a first event—is a passing from *potential* to *actual*. A potential cannot actualize itself. Where, then, does it receive its actuality from?

I confess that the more I observe actual events, the clearer the answer seems to me. The alternative now strikes me as worse than superstition. It is one thing to suppose that an event has a *magical* or *unknown* cause. But to suppose it has no cause or condition whatsoever invites chaos into my mind. My very thoughts and beliefs might then be random and uncaused blips. Yet, if I try to argue that my thoughts have some basis, then my very argument requires causes and effects in my own thinking. Without a principle of cause and effect, I see no rational foundation for any rational thought.

Now to be clear, I do not claim everyone *must*, by psychological law, see that what I say is true. When I was in college, I did not see any of this. I never even considered how "irrelevant differences" could be relevant to a principle of cause and effect. Moreover, even after I had considered this idea, a certain objection (number eight below) blocked me from clear sight. In general, whatever *can* be seen can also be blocked from sight.

On the flipside, just because crowds of people don't see something doesn't mean *you* cannot see it.

To review, there are three ways a mere potential might be actual. First, it might make itself actual. Second, something actual might actualize it. Third, it might be actual without anything making it actual. The first option conflicts with reason: a mere potential would then be both actual (to make itself actual) and not actual (to be made actual). The third option conflicts with experience and the principle of irrelevant differences: a chaos of Disney princesses, and any other mere potentials, never appear from nowhere. That leaves the second option, which fits both reason and experience: only something actual can make a potential actual.

OBJECTION 5: UNCAUSED LAWS

Objection. Some people have suggested to me that perhaps things *can* appear from nowhere, even though we never see this. The reason we never see random blobs appearing from nothing is simply that the actual laws of physics do not allow it. With these laws in place, perhaps nothing new can appear spontaneously from nothing. The basic laws, then, would explain why Spiderman and other characters never snap into existence from nothing. The basic laws preclude widespread chaos. In other words, once something exists—for instance, basic laws—*then* nothing can come from nothing. By contrast, before anything exists, *anything* can happen.

Reply. Reason reveals that some things *cannot* happen. For example, you cannot read these words *without* reading these words. That cannot happen. So *if* the objector is right in thinking that anything *could* happen if there *were* nothing, it follows that there couldn't have been nothing.

To draw out this point, suppose, for sake of argument, that the basic laws are not necessary. Suppose instead they can fail to exist. In this case, it is possible for the laws to *fail* to prevent uncaused chaos.

The laws are like a cage designed to keep fictional characters (and other random blobs) from randomly leaping into our world. But if the laws themselves can randomly fail to exist, then the cage is not secure. The barrier between fiction and reality is then unlocked. An unlocked cage is the same as no cage: in either case, a chaos of random characters *can* escape from fiction at any moment. So why don't they?

How can the universe be secure from a chaos of fictional characters (and other random blobs) from randomly snapping in and out of existence? I see one way: the universe is secure by having laws *whose existence is secure*. These laws—at least some of them—are secure because they have a nature that precludes their non-existence. In other words, the basic laws have a necessary nature: they cannot not exist—which explains why they never *cease* to exist.

In this way, the basic laws provide a firm barrier between the land of fiction (mere potential) and the land of reality (what is actual). The only way out of fiction is to be *released*, and the only way to be released is for something to release it.

This result is precisely what the Principle of Actuality predicts. According to the Principle of Actuality, no mere potential can be actual on its own. From this very principle, it follows that basic, *uncaused* rules of reality were never merely potential. Instead, they are—and have always been—automatically actual.

The Principle of Actuality, then, secures the barrier between fiction and reality. In this way, the Principle of Actuality provides the deepest account of the basic laws themselves. It accounts for how any principle can persist. The principle accounts, in the deepest way, for why mere potentials (whether potential principles or potential particles) never become actual, or cease to be actual, willy nilly. This principle predicts that nothing—no Disney princesses, no random blobs, no laws—appears spontaneously from nothing. This result matches all experience.

Going Deeper

Here is a further reason some rules of reality *cannot* fail to hold. Suppose every rule can fail to hold. Then no rules are necessary. Yet, notice that "no rule is necessary" is then one of the rules. Is this "no necessity" rule itself necessary? If so, then it contradicts itself: for it would then be a necessary rule that no rule is necessary. By reason, then, the "no necessity" rule *cannot* be necessary. But then it is *necessary* that "no necessity" is not necessary. So either way, some rule is necessary.

OBJECTION 6: COST OF COMPLEXITY

Objection. According to Ockham's razor (a principle proposed by William of Ockham), the simplest hypothesis is the most probable, all other things being equal. For example, the hypothesis that a single author wrote these words you are reading here is simpler than the hypothesis that many independent authors wrote these words. The simpler hypothesis shaves off needless complexity and is therefore more plausible. The Foundation Theory, however, multiplies complexity beyond necessity. According to the Foundation Theory, reality divides into *two* kinds: *dependent* and *non-dependent*. That's too many kinds. According to Ockham's razor, we should shave off the non-dependent foundation.

Reply. Sometimes the simplest hypothesis contradicts other things we know. For example, I know that my wife exists. Yet, the hypothesis that the universe includes such a being as *my wife* is not as simple as a hypothesis that posits fewer beings. In this case, I have good reason to think the universe is complex enough to include my wife.

In a similar way, we have good reason to think reality is complex enough to include both the dependent and the non-dependent. For recall the blob of everything. It does not depend on any outside cause or explanation. Thus, by reason alone, a self-sufficient, non-dependent type of reality exists. Otherwise, nothing would exist. The hypothesis that there is nothing is *too simple* to be true.

OBJECTION 7: CONCEIVABILITY OF NOTHING (HUME)

Objection. The philosopher David Hume has debunked all arguments for a necessary foundation. Hume taught us that any existing thing is *conceivably* non-existent.[3] For example, I can conceive of a world with no chairs, no trees, and no universe. Then since conceivability implies possibility, each thing has the real possibility of not existing. A necessary foundation, however, is supposed to have *no* possibility of not existing. Therefore, a necessary foundation contradicts Hume's insight into conceivability.

Reply. There have been developments in logic since Hume's time, and some of those developments are relevant to his concern. In particular, developments in the logic of possibility have clarified a distinction between possibility and mere conceivability. Conceivability does not always imply possibility. For example, I can conceive (in some sense) of a prime number producing a prime minister. Yet, that conception does not reveal the actual powers of a prime number to produce prime ministers. Therefore, the inference from conceivability to possibility is mistaken.

To be more precise, then, we can distinguish between mere "conceptual" possibilities and "ontological" possibilities. Here is what I mean. Let us say something is conceptually possible for you if it is coherent to you, given your actual concepts. Ontological possibilities, by contrast, are not about *you*; they are about the nature of the world. While you might be able to conceive of a world without anything (no foundation, no math, no logic, no possibilities, no principles of reason), this mere conception does absolutely nothing to reveal that the world actually *could* be empty. The basic principles of the world do not hold their breath for you. In other words, the foundation can have a necessary nature independently of what you or I happen to conceive.

I offer one more point: Hume's very assumption about conceivability actually cuts *against* his conclusion. Here is why. It is conceivable that something has a necessary nature, such as a necessarily existent particle or a logical principle. Hume assumes that conceivability implies

[3]D. Hume, *Dialogues Concerning Natural Religion* (Cambridge: Cambridge University Press, 2007 [originally 1779]), 58-59.

possibility. If he were right, then something *could* be necessary (since that is conceivable). Yet since the time of Hume, logicians have developed a rigorous logic of possibility.[4] In this logic, something cannot even be *possibly* necessary unless it is *actually* necessary. The basic reason (without going into technical details) is this: if a necessary thing does *not* exist but could, then the necessary thing would be a mere *potential* thing, which contradicts the nature of a *necessary* thing. Therefore, Hume's own assumption entails that a necessary thing exists after all.

OBJECTION 8: BOOTSTRAPPING (CONTEMPORARY)

Objection. How could a foundation produce anything? The foundation has a *necessary nature*, while its effects do not. So, how can a necessary nature give rise to things that lack a necessary nature?

The problem is with the *link* between a foundation and its effects. Suppose a foundation produces an effect, E. The event of *producing E* is the link between the foundation and E. Call this link "Creation." We now have a dilemma: Creation either has necessary existence or not. Both options cause trouble. If Creation has necessary existence, then *everything* has necessary existence. Surely not everything has necessary existence. Therefore, Creation does not have necessary existence.

But if Creation does not have necessary existence, we have other trouble. By the Principle of Actuality, something must have actualized Creation. What could do that? Things in E cannot actualize Creation because E depends on Creation. That leaves the foundation. Could the foundation create Creation? No. Creation is the link, not the effect. If the foundation creates Creation, then Creation is the *effect*, not the link. Therefore, Creation cannot exist.

Reply. This objection serves to clarify the link between a cause and its effects.

On a basic level, something actualizes an effect by making some potential actual. This basic idea, however, leads to a puzzle about how

---

[4]See J. Garson, *Modal Logic for Philosophers*, 2nd ed. (Cambridge: Cambridge University Press, 2016). This logic of possibility is part of what I mean by "possible" in the context of our inquiry. For motivations for this logic, see A. Pruss and J. Rasmussen, *Necessary Existence* (New York: Oxford University Press, 2018), chap. 2.

anything can make anything actual. Here's the puzzle. Suppose *c* makes *e* actual. We now have three realities: *c*, *e*, and the *event* of *c* making *e* actual. Let's call the event of *c* making *e* actual "*e2*." The puzzle arises when we consider what makes *e2* actual. What caused *e2*? Suppose we say that *c* makes *e2* actual. Then we begin to travel down an infinite regress. We now have the event "*e3*," which is the event of *c* making *e2* actual. By the same reasoning, we have the event "*e4*," which is the event of *c* making *e3* actual. And so on. In general, for every event *en* in the series, there is another event, *en+1*, which is the event of *c* making *en* actual. It then follows that there are infinitely many events involved in the making of every event! How can that be?

Here is one possible answer, which I also think is the correct answer. When *c* actualizes *e*, *c* performs a basic act of actualization. As a result of this basic act, a couple things logically *follow*: (1) *e* is actual, and (2) *c's actualizing e* is actual. These things that follow are not themselves actualized by any basic act of actualization. It is not as though *c* must actualize the state *e is actual* in order to actualize *e*. Rather, *e is actual* is "actualized" in a derivative way. Specifically, *e is actual* is actualized by a combination of *c*'s basic act of actualizing *e* together with logical entailment. There is only *one* basic act of actualization involved here: *c*'s actualizing *e*. Logic does the rest.

The above account applies to Creation. This event consists in the foundation *n* actualizing some event *e*. There is one basic act of actualization here. *N* simply actualizes *e*. Then, by logic, Creation *follows*. We could say, then, that Creation is actualized in a derivative way: Creation is "actualized" by virtue of a combination of *n*'s basic act of actualizing *e* together with logical entailment. No circularity is required.

Thus, rather than destroy the Principle of Actuality, we have sharpened it. The Principle of Actuality predicts that every actuality is either (1) *foundational*—with no potential to not exist—or (2) actualized by something prior. In the case of Creation, the only thing that could be prior is the necessary foundation itself. This foundation "actualizes" Creation *not* by directly actualizing it. Rather, foundation actualizes Creation by directly actualizing some event *e*, and this basic act of actualization then *entails* the existence of Creation. Again, no circularity is required.

I want my answer to get to the *root* of the worry. Therefore, I will conclude my reply with an observation about the root source of this "bootstrapping" objection. This objection, in its various forms, is about the *link* between a necessary foundation and its non-necessary effects. In the twentieth century, several philosophers (notably, William Rowe and Peter van Inwagen) independently articulated a worry about how there could be any such link.[5] Their worry arose in response to certain arguments for a necessary foundation. These arguments seemed to imply that the link between the necessary foundation and its non-necessary (chance or freely selected) effects would itself be necessary or unexplained. Both options are problematic.

The foundation of our bridge has the materials for a complete solution. We have the Principle of Actuality, which leaves open the method and manner of dependence. In particular, this principle allows for both choice and chance: an actualizer may select among several options. As we saw above, an actualizer of *e* need not also perform another act to actualize the *actualization of e*. Instead, it might just actualize *e*, and that's that. This result is favorable: it secures our observations of cause and effect, while solving the bootstrapping problem.

I'd like to close this reply by noting an intriguing consequence of the bootstrapping problem. Instead of exposing a problem with a necessary foundation, it points instead to a *feature* of the necessary foundation. Consider this: if everything is a necessary consequence of the necessary foundation, then everything is necessary, full stop—and so part of the necessary totality. Yet, apparently, *not* everything is necessary, full stop; for example, my current thoughts can fail to exist. If that is right, then the necessary foundation is capable of selecting certain effects *among alternative possibilities*. In this sense, the foundation has a form of "choice."[6]

OBJECTION 9: GAP

Objection. Why think anything exists *beyond* the universe? Maybe the universe is itself the foundation of all dependent realities.

---

[5]W. Rowe, *The Cosmological Argument* (Princeton: Princeton University Press, 1975), 103-11; P. van Inwagen, *An Essay on Free Will* (Oxford: Clarendon, 1983), 202-4.

[6]For one reason to think this "choice" is not explicable in terms of chance, see J. Rasmussen, "From a Necessary Being to God," *Religious Studies* 66, no. 1 (2009): 1-13.

Reply. While we might speculate about what may exist "beyond" the universe, nothing in the bridge of reason up to this point settles that speculation. Our bridge so far takes us to a *foundation*. We have identified some aspects of the foundation: the foundation (1) is independent in nature, (2) is necessary in nature, and (3) provides an account of how there can be anything at all. We will continue to use the tool of reason to see what else we can see about the nature of the foundation. The bridge is not yet complete.

ONE MORE BEAM: THE LOGIC OF POSSIBILITY (EXTRA)

Toward the end of the twentieth century, logicians made some discoveries that are relevant to our bridge. In particular, they developed systems of logic that penetrate the familiar concept of *possibility*. The systems encode basic principles of possibility. From such principles, logicians deduce theorems and discover new insights.

During the development of this new logic, we have seen a corresponding resurgence of interest in a necessary foundation. Philosophers (myself among them) have written academic articles with new arguments in the language of the new logic.[7]

Here I will offer one example to illustrate how we might use the logic of possibility to amplify the Foundation Theory. I present to you the following argument from possibility:

1. Whatever can become actual can possibly be made actual.
2. Nothing can possibly make actuality—the state of something being actual—actual.
3. Therefore, actuality cannot become actual.
4. Actuality is actual (i.e., there are actual things).
5. Therefore, actuality is actual but cannot become actual.
6. If actuality is actual but cannot become actual, then something is actual on its own (in a foundational way).
7. Therefore, something is actual on its own.

[7]For a catalogue of such arguments, see Pruss and Rasmussen, *Necessary Existence*.

Let us examine each step in the argument. The first premise is about possibility: whatever can become actual can possibly be made actual. Let's think about what this premise means. For concreteness, imagine a blue ball. When I say that a blue ball can possibly be made actual, I mean this: it is consistent with the principles of reason for something to make a blue ball actual. For example, the production of a blue ball is possible because such a production does not contradict any principle of reason.

This first premise is very modest. It allows, for sake of argument, uncaused events. For example, perhaps a blue ball could snap into existence from nothing. While I previously argued that no mere potential (such as a potential event) can be actual without a source, I want to draw attention to another, independent route. Instead of *requiring* that a blue ball have a source, the premise here merely says that any genuine potential *can* come from something. In other words, a source of a potential is at the very least *compatible* with reason.

Reason itself testifies to (1). By reason, we can see that potential things *can* have a cause. For example, by reason we can see that *it is consistent with reason* that something causes a potential ball to be actual. The same is so for any potential thing: if something is a genuine potential, then something could—consistent with reason—cause the potential to be actual. Differences in shape or size make no difference. Reason does not discriminate between differences in the potential. As long as the thing is a genuine potential, it is consistent with reason that something causes the potential to be actual. This consistency with reason is itself a principle of reason.

We are now ready for premise (2): nothing can possibly make *actuality* actual. The reason is that to make something actual presupposes that something is actual. To illustrate, suppose a particle named Bob wants to make *actuality* actual. It's too late. Bob is already actual. In other words, actuality—the state of there being something actual—is already actual. In general, no *actual* thing can make *actuality* actual.

In fact, we can deduce premise (2) from the law of non-contradiction. Here is how. To make actuality actual requires that something make itself actual. But as we saw in my response to objection four, something can only make itself actual if it can be actual and non-actual. Again, if something makes itself actual, then this something would already be actual without *yet* being actual—a contradiction. Fortunately, there is a way to be free from this contradiction: accept premise (2).

These steps take us to (3): *therefore*, actuality cannot become actual. Again, if actuality could *become* actual, then actuality could be *made* actual—by premise (1). We have seen that nothing actual can make actuality itself actual (otherwise we have a contradiction). Therefore, actuality cannot become actual. Still with me?

Next, we observe that actuality *is actual*. To say that actuality is actual is to say that *something or other* is actual. For example, you are actual. Therefore, actuality—the state of there being something—is actual.

The result is this: actuality is actual, yet actuality did not *become* actual. There is only one way actuality could be actual without becoming actual. That way is this: something has actuality *on its own*, without becoming actual.

To draw out the result, consider how actuality can exist at all. There are three options: (1) actuality (the state of something being actual) makes itself actual; (2) something other than actuality makes actuality actual; and (3) nothing makes actuality actual. Options (1) and (2) both entail that something actual exists prior to all actual things, which is a contradiction. So that leaves (3): nothing makes actuality actual. In other words, actuality is actual on its own, without a source.

This result takes us once again to the foundation of the world. Recall that the foundation is actual on its own. By having a foundation in place, then, we have an anchor for actuality. Actuality is actual, without a source, because the foundation is actual and without a source.

This result shines light on actuality using the logic of possibility. You might initially wonder how the logic of possibility could tell us anything about something *actual*. How does seeing a possibility help us see an actuality? Part of the answer is that we don't start with *mere* possibility. We start with something actual—like you, and logic itself. We then use reason to make deductions. We deduce, from irrelevant differences, that mere potentials can—without contradicting any rule of reason—be made actual (recall premise [1]). Next, we deduce, from the law of non-contradiction, that nothing can make actuality actual—since actuality would then already be actual (recall premise [2]). From these results, we deduce that actuality was never a mere potential.

We can deduce an even more exciting result. The foundation is not only the foundation for the actual things. It is also the foundation for all *possible* things. That is because the foundation cannot be a mere potential thing. Potential things are only actual if they depend on a source, yet the foundation has no source. Therefore, the foundation is not, and cannot be, a mere potential thing. Instead, the foundation is, and must be, actual. For this reason, the foundation of everything is a foundation for both the actual and the possible.[8]

SUMMARY

We investigated the foundation of our bridge with the instrument of objections. The objections serve us by clarifying concepts. The objections do not cause our bridge to collapse. Rather, they help us probe the integrity of each of our support beams.

You may still have questions. That is to be expected. Continue to test the bridge. Test everything. Be skeptical, cautious, and careful. It is the way to see more.

---

[8]If you would like to explore these concepts further, see necessarybeing.com. I created this website to help people test several pathways that lead to a foundation with a necessary nature. The website contains a survey, which collects information about what seems true to those who take the survey. Interestingly, it turns out that the vast majority of those who are initially skeptical of a necessary foundation—including a majority of philosophy professors—give reports that entail, by logic alone, that there is a necessary foundation (Pruss and Rasmussen, *Necessary Existence*, chap. 1).

CHAPTER 5

ETERNAL POWER

Power is the capacity to produce an effect. For example, a car has the power to crash into a building. The effect is a broken car. An orange tree has the power to produce oranges. A police officer has the power to give you a ticket. And so on.

In this brief chapter, I will use my powers to build the next step on our bridge. I shall show how the foundation of our bridge supports a step to a special sort of power: this power is eternal.

EXTENDING THE BRIDGE

In the previous chapters, I built a bridge of reason that supports steps to the following result: there is a foundation of things. This foundation exists without any outside cause or outside explanation. It has within itself the capacity to exist on its own.

I will now install the next piece of the bridge. This piece will give us the power to see something about the foundation's *power*.

I start with an observation: power exists. You have the power to keep reading, for example. Scientists have the power to discover new aspects of our universe. Inventors have the power to develop new technologies. And so on. Even if everything is an illusion, you have the power to consider whether everything is an illusion. You have the power to produce effects in your own mind.

Next, a question: how did power come to exist? Why does any power exist at all?

Logic reveals exactly two options:

Option 1: Power ultimately came into existence from nothing.

Option 2: Power never came into existence.

To help us think about these options, let us imagine first that there was a time without any power. Imagine, for example, blank, empty space. In this blank space, nothing has the capacity to produce any effects. Furthermore, nothing has the capacity to produce *power.*

The empty space scenario is perplexing: if nothing has the capacity to produce power, how can power ever *enter* into the world? Perhaps we can conceive of power snapping into existence without any prior power. But conceivability is not the same as possibility. We can conceive (in some sense) of a prime number giving birth to a prime minister, but such a birth is impossible. Similarly, while the "power from nowhere" may be conceivable (in some sense), it does not follow that it is possible.

But suppose, for sake of argument, power did appear from nothing, without anything actualizing the power. Then we face a puzzle: why doesn't *any* power of *any* magnitude enter or exit reality *any* place at *any* time? What stops that? Maybe this: a Grand Power stops new powers from randomly entering or exiting reality. Perhaps this Grand Power is part of the fabric of our universe. This proposal solves nothing, however. How does this Grand Power manage to remain in existence? Why doesn't it randomly disappear? Is there a Super Grand Power that stops the Grand Power from leaving our world? If there is a Super Grand Power, what stops the Super Grand Power from disappearing? What stops *all* powers together—whatever they are—from spontaneously exiting reality at once?

Only one kind of power could prevent a chaos of random powers from popping in and out of existence. This power is a power that cannot *itself* pop in or out of existence. It is a power that exists on its own, by its own nature. Power from nothing, by contrast, falls off the rails of reason laid in the previous chapters (see especially chapter four, objection four).

What sort of power could exist on its own? The previous parts of our bridge include the materials for an answer. A power that exists on its own has an *independent nature*, and its independent nature springs from its *necessary existence*. The foundation of all power, then, is a *necessarily existent* power.[1]

A necessarily existent power cannot come to exist or cease to exist. Suppose power begins to exist. Then prior to its beginning, it doesn't exist. Similarly, if power ceases to exist, then posterior to its ceasing, it doesn't exist. Either way, some state of the world obtains without the power's existence. Yet a *necessary* power exists no matter what state of the world obtains. So, a necessary power never begins to exist or ceases to exist. In that sense, the power is eternal.[2]

The foundational power, then, is another feature of the foundation of existence. So far, we have seen that the foundation has the following features: (1) independence, (2) necessary existence, and (3) ultimacy. We can now add another feature to the list: a foundation has (4) eternal power.

Suppose, instead, the foundation lacks eternal power. Then either the foundation has no power ever, or it begins to have power. In either case, power enters reality *from nothing*. But by reason and universal experience (and the principles comprising the foundation of our bridge), power doesn't enter (or exit) reality from nothing. Instead, the foundation's power never begins (or ceases). Its power is eternal.

CLARIFYING THE STRUCTURE

A friend of mine with whom I discussed these ideas offered me a couple of questions. These questions are valuable because they serve to clarify the intended structure of my bridge. Thus, I will address them here.

Question 1. If the foundation has eternal power, where did this power get *its* power?

Answer. The short answer is that the foundation didn't *get* its power.

To draw out why, consider that there are two possible types of things: (1) things that can fail to be, and (2) things that *cannot* fail to

---

[1]We could say the foundational power exists *a se* ("of itself"). See M. Davidson, "God and Other Necessary Beings," *Stanford Encyclopedia of Philosophy* (2013), https://plato.stanford.edu/entries/god-necessary-being/.

[2]For the purposes of this book, I leave open the nature of time. Some philosophers endorse *eternalism*, which is the position that whatever exists at any time also exists *simpliciter*. For example, dinosaurs that *did* exist also exist simpliciter. If eternalism is true, then the foundation's power is eternal in at least this sense: there is no time at which the foundation's power began or ceased to exist *simpliciter*.

be. In chapter three, I explained why I think the foundation is something that cannot fail to be. It has a necessary nature. Now whatever has a necessary nature cannot be brought *into* existence from non-existence. In other words, the foundation cannot itself come into existence from non-existence.

The same reasoning applies to the *power* of the foundation. The foundational power cannot itself come into existence from non-existence. Nor can the foundational power depend upon any source of power, for that would be circular. Therefore, the foundational power must be a self-existent power. This power simply *is*. It exists on its own without any source.

Question 2. How can anything be *eternal*? For example, if the foundation of existence is eternal, how long did the foundation wait before making our universe? Forever? What was it doing?

Answer. I am aware of exactly two ways to be eternal. One way is to exist for infinitely many moments without a first or last moment (i.e., *everlastingness*). The other way is to be timeless (i.e., *atemporal eternity*). Both ways have something in common: an eternal being doesn't *become* actual or *cease to be* actual. These two ways of being eternal lead to two ways in which a foundation can be eternal. Here is one way: the foundation has no beginning or end in time. Here is the other: the foundation is timeless.

Going Deeper

Here is a third option: the foundation is timeless without the existence of time. When time exists, on the other hand, the foundation is temporal. On this account, time depends on the foundation: without the foundation's creation, there is no time—and the foundation is timeless.

Fortunately, we don't need to figure out the actual length of time for our purposes. Instead, we can see how the foundation would be eternal on any theory of time. There are three options to consider: (1) time has a beginning, (2) time doesn't have a beginning, or (3) time is merely a fiction of your mind.

Consider each option in turn. On option (1), the foundation does not *become* actual at the first moment; it just *is* actual. Like a finger that causes water to begin to ripple, the foundation causes time to begin to flow. On option (2), the foundation has existed from eternity past, perhaps creating infinitely many universes along the way, or the foundation is altogether timeless. On option (3), everything is timeless, since time is not real.

Personally, I find option (1) to be the most plausible. In any case, it doesn't matter: we don't need to figure out which option is correct to see how the foundation would be eternal on any of the conceivable options.

SUMMARY

The foundational power is eternal: it never became actual and will never cease to be actual. If instead the foundational power *became* actual, then something must have the power to actualize the foundational power. In that case, there would be a power before there is power—a contradiction. The only kind of power, then, that can be foundational is a power that is incapable of entering or exiting reality—that is, an eternal power.

CHAPTER 6

PURELY ACTUAL

It is time for the next step. In previous chapters, we used the tool of reason to construct steps to an ultimate foundation of things. By probing the foundation, we uncovered several features: independence, necessity, ultimacy, and eternal power. The next step is about another feature. This one is *deeper in*.

Here is a preview of what is coming. We will peer into the foundation. To help us explore, I will use three reason-based tools. They have the following names: (1) simplicity, (2) explanatory depth, and (3) uniformity. Each tool will independently reveal the same thing from a different angle. Each tool has its own power, which we can use to construct the next step.

Few people on earth have seen the step I am about to lay down. I myself had no idea it was possible to see this much. I had no idea reason had the power to reveal this much. Even after I began to see the works of reason, I didn't understand the true nature of reason or the source of its power. That understanding came later.

As we peer into the foundation, we will find a certain *fullness*. This fullness touches every feature of the foundation. Every feature is fully actualized, without arbitrary cut-offs. The ultimate layer of everything has no gaps, holes, spots, blips, boundaries, wrinkles, or arbitrary limits of any kind. Instead, by the three tools, we will see a foundation that is full, complete, and purely actual.[1]

Allow me to explain.

[1]What follows clarifies Aquinas's proposal that the first being (i.e., the foundation) has no potentiality. Thomas Aquinas, *Summa theologiae*, trans. Fathers of the English Dominican Province (New York: Benzinger, 1948), I.3.1.

THREE TOOLS TO PROBE THE FOUNDATION

Tool 1: Simplicity. First, simpler theories are more probable, *other things being equal.* To illustrate, suppose you walk outside, and everything you see is wet. Trees. Grass. Roads. All are wet. What explains your observation of wetness? Here is a familiar hypothesis: *it rained last night.* Seems sensible. But other hypotheses can explain the observations. Consider, for example, this hypothesis: some boy put buckets of water on the sidewalks, sprinklers got water on the grass, and thousands of birds spit water on the leaves. This hypothesis also explains your observations. This explanation is as thorough as the rain hypothesis. It explains *all* the data. But which hypothesis is more probable?

Other things being equal, the *simpler* hypothesis is more probable. The simpler hypothesis is *internally* more probable. The rain hypothesis is simpler than the boy-sprinklers-birds hypothesis. Therefore, the rain hypothesis is more probable (other things being equal).

To be clear, a less-probable hypothesis *could* still be true. After all, it could turn out that some kid put buckets of water on the sidewalks. Even still, the simpler hypothesis is internally *more likely*, other things being equal.

Why is a simpler hypothesis more likely? This question may seem like a deep and unanswerable philosophical question. But just because people puzzle over a question does not mean it has no answer. I will offer an answer that I think one can see by the light of reason.

The answer—the reason the simpler hypothesis is more internally probable—is that the simpler hypothesis includes less total information and so has fewer ways to go wrong. To illustrate, suppose you have two hypotheses A and B. Suppose, next, that A is composed of basic parts, *a1* and *a2* and *a3*, while B is composed of just *b1* and *b2*. Then A has three "opportunities" to be false, while B has only two. Now suppose you have *no idea* whether any of the components of A or B are true, and you have no idea whether the truth of one component depends on the truth of any other. Each component is equally plausible in your mind. Then, from where you stand, B is more probable than A because B has fewer components—and so fewer opportunities to be false.

Going Deeper

The complexity of a hypothesis flows from the quantity of basic components within it, not the quantity of words used to express it. Consider, for example, the following hypotheses: (1) "Adam is a bachelor" and (2) "Adam is a male." Both hypotheses have four words. Still, the word *bachelor* contains more information than the word *male*. In fact, the concept of a bachelor includes the concept of a male plus the concept of being unmarried. For this reason, hypothesis (1) is more complicated than hypothesis (2). Simplicity, then, is not about how many words you use. Rather, it is about how many basic concepts are involved. The fewer the basic concepts, the simpler the proposition.

This preference for simplicity helps scientific investigation. In the scientific context, some call the preference for simplicity "Ockham's razor" (after William of Ockham). The idea is that we should not multiply entities beyond necessity because doing so diminishes the probability of our hypothesis. For example, the law of gravity explains why we see apples fall to the earth. Yet here is a different explanation: an invisible flying spaghetti monster chooses to move apples to the earth whenever they drop. The gravity proposal is simpler: it posits fewer assumptions. Therefore, it is internally more likely.

Here is why simplicity is relevant to our inquiry: we can use Ockham's razor to trim less-probable theories of the foundation. People have proposed many theories about the nature of ultimate reality. According to Ockham's razor, the simplest one is the most probable, other things being equal. A theory that posits unnecessary complexity, by contrast, has more "opportunities" to be false. So, if you want to increase your chance of getting truth, seek the *simplest* theory that accounts for the data.

Let us take an obvious example of an improbable theory. Consider the *Disney princess* hypothesis: the ultimate foundation of reality has the exact shape of a Disney princess. Imagine that, just prior to the birth of our universe, the only thing that exists is an object that looks exactly like a Disney princess. Suddenly, this object jerks. *Snap!* A Big Bang occurs, and the princess-shaped object spews out our universe.

This hypothesis is conceivable (in some sense). Is it *true*? Not likely. By Ockham's razor alone, the Disney princess hypothesis is internally improbable. It is improbable because it posits needless complexity. Specifically, the Disney princess hypothesis posits a Disney princess shape. A princess shape includes many other shapes, like the shape of ears and the shape of a nose. Each of these shapes contributes to the complexity of the hypothesis, which in turn contributes to its improbability. The Disney princess hypothesis is not probable because it is not simple. This result rings of truth.

One more example. You may have heard it said that a *supernatural* being produced the universe. Is this proposal probable? Well, consider that according to Ockham's razor, any theory that posits extra complexity is *less likely* to be true, other things being equal. A supernatural being is an extra kind of being: *super*-natural. It would be simpler if all beings alike had the same uniform nature—*natural*—would it not? If so, then the "supernatural" hypothesis is less likely to be true, other things being equal.

In view of the title of this book, you might be surprised to hear me say that the "supernatural" hypothesis is less likely (other things being equal). But hear me: *I am following reason where it leads*. Reason leads me to this result. So, I follow reason to this result. (That is not to say that the most probable theory is automatically the correct theory. We will look deeper to see what theory may provide the best explanation, all things considered.)

To be clear, while the bridge will take us to a foundation that is special (as we shall see), we do not need to stumble over whether to call the foundation "natural" or "supernatural." The term *supernatural* is variable in meaning, and it invites an unnecessary obstacle to our destination. In fact, when we reach the end, we will see that, in some sense, the foundation is the *most natural* of all possible things. The foundation is not *beyond* all that we know. Rather, the foundation *anchors* all that we know. I want to show how we can reach this result without stumbling over words.

My project, as you know, is to build a bridge that can serve the greatest number of people possible. For this reason, I seek to use the most inclusive materials. When I use principles, such as the principle of simplicity, I only make use of them if they have a good reputation among philosophers from many, divergent perspectives. Rather than use cheap plastic, I endeavor to build this bridge with the finest gold.

In summary, we can use the principle of simplicity to investigate the foundation. With this tool in hand, we can compare theories: a theory that posits needless complexity is internally less probable than a simpler theory. The simpler is more probable.

Tool 2: Explanatory depth. Next, we have reason to favor theories that have *explanatory depth*. Recall the rain hypothesis: rain can explain why the trees are wet. Here is a different hypothesis: *nothing* explains why things are wet. Instead, the wetness appeared from nowhere, without any cause or explanation. Which hypothesis do you think is more probable: that it rained, or that the wetness came from nothing? Surely, the rain hypothesis is more probable.

Yet notice that rain adds complexity. The wet-from-*nothing* hypothesis is simpler. So why isn't the simpler hypothesis more probable?

Simplicity is not the only thing to consider. Suppose the wet came from nothing. Then the wet lacks an *explanation* altogether. But surely wetness has some explanation. The rain hypothesis has this advantage, then: it provides an explanation of the wetness. In other words, the rain hypothesis provides greater explanatory depth.

Explanatory depth is a powerful tool. To see its power in action, I want to show how it can solve a classic problem that threatens all scientific inquiry. This problem, originally posed by David Hume, is about how we can know anything based on past observations.[2] Consider that today is a new day. Never in the history of the world before today has today occurred. Therefore, never in the history of the world has rain explained *today*'s wetness. The experience of the past does not include the experience of the present. But then how can previous experiences tell us anything about *present* reality?

This question might seem too deep to be answerable. Yet I think an answer is possible. I would be dishonest if I pretended otherwise. I must be honest: I think reason reveals a solution.

Here is my solution. By reason, we can see three things about the rain hypothesis *in the present*: first, we can see that the rain hypothesis is

[2]See L. Henderson, "The Problem of Induction," *Stanford Encyclopedia of Philosophy* (2018), https://plato.stanford.edu/entries/induction-problem.

relatively simple (and so relatively probable); second, we can see that the rain hypothesis can account for our previous experiences (or our present memories of them); third, we can see that the rain hypothesis predicts today's wetness. By these three things, we can then infer a *probabilistic connection* between the past and the present. In this way, we can infer that the present probably resembles the past.

This same reasoning illustrates the value of explanatory depth. Consider the following hypothesis: whatever exists has some explanation (i.e., it didn't come into existence from nothing). Reason reveals three things about this hypothesis: first, it is relatively simple (and so relatively probable); second, it can account for our previous experiences (or memories of them); and third, it predicts that whatever exists has some explanation, no matter what day it is. By these three things, we can then infer a *probabilistic connection* between existing things and some explanation for their existence.

To be extra safe, we can work with the modest hypothesis that existing things probably have some explanation, other things being equal. In other words, there is a presumption in favor of an explanation. For example, if you encounter a blue sphere, you can expect there to be some explanation for its existence, even if you have no idea what it is.

We can use this principle of explanation to probe the foundation. I'll give one example here to illustrate. Consider the theory that the foundation has the shape of a *telephone pole*. This telephone pole theory is obviously not the best. The problem is not *only* that a telephone pole is arbitrarily complex. Complexity is one problem. Here is another problem: the telephone hypothesis lacks explanatory depth. It leaves unexplained why the foundation happens to have the precise shape of a telephone pole. A theory in which the foundation provides an *ultimate* explanation for all shaped objects has greater explanatory depth than a theory that leaves the existence of some shaped objects unexplained.

Moreover, consider this. All theories of reality fall into two categories. Either the theory has simplicity at the foundation, or it has some arbitrary degree of complexity at the foundation. A theory that has simplicity at the foundation provides a *foundation* for complexity. The complexity of all the arbitrary limits that ever come to exist then ultimately arises from the simple foundation. If instead arbitrary complexity is at the foundation of things, then the foundation has arbitrary limits without any explanation.

In summary, explanatory depth helps guide us toward the *best* explanation. When comparing theories, we can ask which theory explains more. We can also ask which theory is simpler. Having a theory that exhibits *both* simplicity and depth is hard to come by, yet the more a theory explains, the more support there is for the theory.

Tool 3: Uniformity. The previous tools—simplicity and explanatory depth—provide probability. I believe the tool I will describe now has the power to provide *direct sight*.

This tool is about *uniformity*. Some categories of things are uniform in a certain respect. For example, all prime numbers are uniform with respect to being a number. They are also uniform in their inability to produce a person. The size of the prime makes no difference. We can see clearly—with *certainty*—that all prime numbers, no matter their size, are uniformly unable to produce a person. We can see this uniformity by seeing the nature of numbers.

To illustrate uniformity further, consider another example. Suppose you want to build a glass tower out of Play-Doh. You will not succeed. Play-Doh is the wrong material. It does not matter how much Play-Doh you have in hand. The amount makes no difference. You can be certain that all the Play-Doh in the world is unable to produce a glass tower. Play-Doh is uniformly unable to produce glass.

We can use a principle of uniformity to probe the foundation. Recall the theory that the foundation has the shape of a telephone pole. We already saw two problems with this theory: (1) it is needlessly complex, and (2) it lacks explanatory depth. There is yet another problem. Shapes have a certain uniformity. All shapes depend on prior causes for their instantiation. If some clay is cubical, its cubical shape came from something, such as hands molding the clay into a cube. All shapes are like that. All come from something. While shapes differ in angles and number of vertices, these differences are irrelevant to the ability to come from nothing. Shapes of things are uniformly dependent on prior causes or states.

To draw out the significance of uniform dependence, suppose the foundational layer of everything had the shape of a telephone pole. That shape, like every other shape, must be dependent. Yet the ultimate fundamental layer, by definition, is independent. Its basic features, therefore, are not dependent. By reason, then, we can infer that a telephone pole shape cannot be a basic feature of the foundation.

To see this same result from another angle, recall that certain principles at the foundation of our bridge entail that the foundation has a *necessary nature*. This nature is as necessary as the principles of reason themselves, since the foundation exists as long as anything exists, including any principles of reason. (I will say more about the relationship between the foundation's nature and reason in chapter ten, "Foundation of Reason.")

The particular shapes of things, by contrast, do not have a necessary nature. Suppose the foundation had the particular shape of a telephone pole. Why would it have *that* shape? Why not some other shape, like the shape of some shoes? The problem here is that a telephone pole shape is not relevantly different from every other shape. The principles of reason do not demand that *any* particular telephones exist; logic is not that specific. Principles of reason may entail that *some* necessary foundation exists, but they do not entail that any *particular* shape characterizes the foundation. It is a requirement of reason that no particular shape is a requirement of reason. If that is right, then while the foundation is necessary, shapes are uniformly non-necessary.

All three tools, then, help us probe the foundation. By the tool of simplicity, we have reason to consider simpler hypotheses about the foundation to be more probable. By the tool of explanatory depth, we have reason to think the foundation provides the deepest possible explanation of things. By the tool of uniformity, we have reason to think the foundation is uniformly different from the non-foundation.

THE PROBLEM OF ARBITRARY LIMITS

With the three tools—simplicity, explanatory depth, and uniformity—we can see something even more profound. We can see something about the foundation's *arbitrary limits*. It has none.

An arbitrary limit is a cutoff without an explanation. For example, if the foundation has a capacity to produce 2^{88} particles and no more, then its capacity to produce particles has a cutoff, and so is limited. This limit is arbitrary.

One might think that any foundation would have some arbitrary limits—such as some particular quantity of energy or mass. However, a foundation with arbitrary limits leads to a threefold problem. Our three tools reveal this problem from three angles. First, each unexplained limit multiplies complexity within the foundation (which detracts from the probability of a hypothesis about the foundation's nature). Second, each limit blocks explanatory depth by adding another unexplained bit to the foundation. Third, each limit within the foundation breaks the uniformity of limits more generally.

Let us look closer at each aspect of this problem. Start with the problem of complexity. Imagine the foundation has the following basic attributes: (1) a mass of 2^{41} grams, (2) the shape of a sphere, and (3) the capacity to produce exactly 2^{88} particles. These attributes are limits—cutoffs—with respect to mass, shape, and capacity. Each cutoff adds complexity to a theory of the basic nature of the foundation, since each cutoff requires additional information to describe that nature. This added complexity reduces the probability of this theory of the foundation.

A simpler theory would be one that doesn't specify any cutoffs. For example, imagine a foundation with these basic attributes: (1) no mass, (2) no shape, and (3) the capacity to produce any number of particles. This theory requires fewer basic attributes and is simpler to describe: the foundation's basic nature could then be described without listing any of these limits. By the tool of simplicity, then, a theory of a limitless foundation is more internally likely than the more complex theory above. In other words, the tool of simplicity provides a reason to think the foundation lacks arbitrary limits. (If it has any complexity, it won't be arbitrary or inexplicable.)

Consider next the problem of explanatory depth, which is another problem for an arbitrarily limited foundation. The problem here is that if the foundation has arbitrary limits, then the foundation (or a *theory* of the foundation) has less power to explain the things that depend on it. Recall the theory just given: the foundation has (1) a mass of 2^{41} grams, (2) the shape of a sphere, and (3) the capacity to produce exactly 2^{88}

particles. Focus on its mass. What might explain the fact that the foundation has a mass of *exactly* 2^{41} grams?

Nothing could explain *foundational* mass in principle. So, if mass is both foundational and unexplained, then the existence of massive objects is unexplained. In this case, mass has no ultimate explanation. On the other hand, if mass has an ultimate explanation, then the foundation must itself have the capacity to explain *all* the massive objects.

The result is general: the deepest explanation of the limits of things (like mass and shape) will be in terms of a foundation that has the capacity to explain all limits whatsoever. If instead the foundation has *unexplained* limits itself, then the foundation obviously cannot *explain* all limits. It follows, by reason, that the deepest explanation of limits would lack unexplained limits.[3]

At this level of depth, you may feel a bit uneasy. Is it genuinely possible to see something so far-reaching about the foundation? How can we be sure our steps are secure?

I hope to bring you some assurance by showing how all three tools each independently point us to the same result. We are now ready to pick up our third tool: *uniformity*. I believe this tool is the most powerful among the three. It has the power to show that arbitrary limits are worse than improbable. By uniformity, arbitrary limits are impossible.

To illustrate the problem exposed by uniformity, imagine a mountain range. This mountain range has a particular shape along its mountaintops. No matter the shape, it has some explanation: for example, it has its shape because of the way certain materials came together via erosion and patterns of wind and water. Whether the mountain range has two peaks or two thousand peaks, its shape does not appear from nothing.

This understanding of the mountain range illustrates a general principle of uniformity. We can see, clearly, that mere *differences in shape* between the mountains are irrelevant to their dependence on some

---

[3]This result is compatible with the foundation having certain *explained* limits. For example, according to trinitarian theology, the foundation includes precisely *three* centers of awareness or personalities. While the number three is a limit, Swinburne proposes an explanation in terms of the highest love. Whether his proposal works or not, the point here is that any limits would need to have a deeper explanation. R. Swinburne, *The Christian God* (Oxford: Oxford University Press, 1994), 343-45.

outside explanation. It is no easier for the limited shape of a two-peak mountain, say, to be independent and uncaused than for the limited shape of a two-thousand-peak mountain shape. The number of peaks is irrelevant. We can see this irrelevance clearly by reason itself.

Let us zoom out to see if we can spot the underlying principle at work in our thinking about the mountain range. Here is what I think I see. The principle about shapes is deducible from a more basic principle about limits: mere *differences in limits* are categorically uniform, whereas a difference with respect to dependence is not categorically uniform. To illustrate, consider a four-gram pile of sugar. This amount of sugar is dependent; four grams of sugar will not appear from nothing. The same is true for *forty* grams. A mere change in amount is completely irrelevant. It is no easier for a four-gram pile of sugar to appear from nothing than a forty-gram pile of sugar. The uniformity of limits makes sense of why: *limits*, all limits, are uniform with respect to their dependence on outside explanations.

Uniformity of dependence springs from uniformity of category. Limits are categorically alike. By contrast, dependence is a category away from non-dependence. Therefore, all limits alike are uniformly dependent.

At this point, you might wonder how anything, whether limited *or not*, could enjoy an *independent* nature. Hold on to this question. When we reach the final step on the bridge of reason, I will identify a root feature that makes sense of independence. We will see that this root feature is not itself a limit but in fact *precludes* all arbitrary limits—and so predicts the same result we are reaching now.

In any case, we do not need to get ahead of ourselves to appreciate the main point here. The point here is this: limits are categorically alike. All are dependent. Mere differences in limits do not make a difference with respect to the ability to be independent. By the twin testimonies of reason and universal experience, limits are uniformly dependent.[4]

[4]Graham Oppy expressed to me the hypothesis that a limit of the foundation might be *independent* in virtue of having necessary existence. This hypothesis serves to clarify the principle of uniformity at work. To my mind, the hypothesis that certain limits have necessary existence relocates the problem. What makes one limit relevantly different from another? You might think that, in general, pure limits mark a boundary between one potential reality (such as a large mountain) and some greater potential reality (such as a larger mountain). For the sake of modesty, my proposal here is wider open: *either* limits ascribable to the foundation are

Going Deeper

What about mathematical limits, like the limited number of sides in a triangle? What could explain these limits? Anything? If not, then are mathematical limits independent, unlike the limits of a mountain range? My answer is that mathematical limits can have an explanation in terms of more basic mathematical principles and definitions. For example, the definition of a triangle ("a closed figure with three sides") explains why its number of sides is not zero or infinite. The limits expressed by a definition are limits expressed by our concepts, not limits of the foundation itself. If triangles, squares, and other shapes exist in an abstract, mathematical realm, this mathematical realm *in total* is infinite and unlimited. I will say more about the foundation of mathematics in chapter ten.

Here, then, is the result so far. All limits alike have an outside explanation upon which they depend. Yet the basic features of the foundation, by contrast, lack an outside explanation. Therefore, the basic features of the foundation have no limits.

If you still feel unsure, it is understandable. We are looking *deeply* into the depths. For this reason, I offer you one further consideration. This consideration is about the big picture. Let us widen our scope and consider reality as a whole.

We can sort *all* theories of reality into two categories: either the theory entails the simplest foundation consistent with reason, or it entails some additional complexity. I will call theories that entail the simplest foundation "trunk theories." According to a trunk theory, reality is like a tree with a single trunk. On this picture, all arbitrary limits and complexities are like leaves and branches, which have their ultimate explanation in terms of something deeper and more unified, like the trunk.

---

uniformly not necessary, or if any such limit *were* somehow necessary, then it would have some deeper explanation within the nature of the foundation itself. Compare: either a purple unicorn is not necessary, or if it *were* somehow necessary, its purple color and unicorn shape would—like every other color and shape—have a deeper explanation.

Contrast trunk theories with every other theory. To illustrate other theories, imagine a tumbleweed, with many twisted branches that scatter endlessly or arbitrarily. On this picture, reality as whole has no *unified* ultimate explanation. Instead, things bottom out in an arbitrary plurality of disparate, unexplained things, like many tangled twigs.

I would like to draw your attention to three reasons to prefer a trunk theory over a tumbleweed theory. These reasons, as you might expect, correspond with our three tools: simplicity, explanatory depth, and uniformity.

First, by the tool of simplicity, trunk theories enable a more probable theory of the basic nature of the foundation. (I will spell out a very specific theory in chapter eleven, once all the steps are in place.)

Second, trunk theories provide greater explanatory depth: the simplest foundation explains the most complexity, since all complexity is then explained by a simple root.

Third, a simple foundation maintains the uniformity of dependence: by reason and experience, every complex array of limits, whether big or small, depends on an outside explanation, whereas the basic nature of the foundation does not.

In summary, a simple ("trunk") foundation provides the *simplest, deepest,* and *most unified* account of all the complexities and particularities we see "above" the foundation.

Over the next three chapters, I will say more about how a foundation could explain various complexities (including material and moral complexities). These explanations will fill out the implications of a complete ("purely actual") nature. I will show how a simple, non-arbitrary, non-limited foundation can be the ultimate foundation of everything else, including material complexities and their limits. I hope that as you continue along, you will see with greater clarity how everything can spring from a singular, unified foundation.

SUMMARY

To help us in our investigation, I have offered three tools: (1) simplicity, (2) explanatory depth, and (3) uniformity. Each tool gives us power to see into the foundation from a unique angle. Simplicity helps us see that simpler theories of the foundation are more probable, other things being equal. Explanatory depth helps us see the value of having a foundation that provides the deepest possible explanation. Finally, uniformity helps us see which account of the foundation sets the foundation apart from non-foundational things, like cubes and clay, that uniformly depend on an outside explanation.

All three tools independently point in the same direction: they point to a simple—"purely actual"—foundation. Simplicity shaves off needless complexity, including arbitrary shapes, gaps, vertices, and so on. Explanatory depth reveals how a simple foundation can explain the most. Finally, the principle of uniformity reveals that a self-sufficient foundation must be unlike the tumbleweed of arbitrary limits, which are uniformly not self-sufficient. Together, then, all three tools point to a common core property: unity. The foundation has a simple, unified nature: it has no gaps, holes, spots, blips, boundaries, wrinkles, or arbitrary limits of any kind.

CHAPTER 7

FOUNDATION OF MIND

This chapter marks a significant milestone in our journey. Explorers who wander upon the bridge of reason may start with diverse ideas about the nature of the world, and they may speculate about the implications of the steps that I've laid down so far. But now we've reached a point where the destination can begin to come into view.

Consider the steps up to this point. The first step was about existence. Something exists. Next, we saw that nothing is outside all existence. Thus, nothing outside existence caused or explained existence. Instead, existence has no outside cause or explanation. The next step was about the foundation of existence. Existence has a foundation, which provides an ultimate basis for the existence of dependent things. Several steps in the bridge underwrite several attributes of the foundation: the foundation is (1) independent (chapter three); (2) necessary (chapters three and four), (3) eternally powerful (chapter five), and (4) purely actual—without arbitrary gaps or limits (chapter six).

Here is a preview of the steps to come. Over the course of the next four chapters, I will install four steps about the foundation's *connection* to an aspect of the world. The first is about the foundation's connection to minds. The second is about its connection to matter. The third is about its connection to ethics. The fourth is about the foundation's connection to reason itself. Each of the four steps takes us across, at its own angle, a certain *mind-like* aspect of the foundation.

Then, in chapter eleven, I will put into place my favorite and final piece of the bridge. It is an archway with inner lights. Each light displays the *deepest* aspect of the foundation. These lights shine on the most foundational feature of the foundation's nature.

As usual, I invite you to test each step along the path. I will get the materials in place and set up the structure, but, ultimately, you are the owner of this investigation. You will get the most out of each step if you participate in the building process. See how the pieces fit with your unique reflection.

A WORLD WITH MINDS

What sort of being are *you*? Here is a clue: you are capable of thinking, feeling, and making decisions. In other words, you have a *conscious mind.*

Minds are strange. Why do any minds exist? We can easily imagine a world without minds. For example, imagine a world that has all the shapes and structures of our universe, except with no emotions, no thoughts, no hopes, and no feelings. Or imagine an evolutionary process that spawns an army of machines shaped nearly like us, yet without any consciousness.

Yet our world manifestly includes conscious minds. *How*? *Why*?

Throughout recorded history, people have provided precisely two fundamentally different accounts of the origin of minds. First, there is the "foundational mind" hypothesis. According to this hypothesis, mental reality is foundational to the rest of reality.[1]

The other account of minds is "materialism." On this hypothesis, the foundation is mindless. Given materialism, *people*—assuming they exist—are the product of a complex pattern of particles, and nothing more. If materialism is true, then reality proceeds from shapes to sensations, from motions to mind, and from particles to people.

As you may expect, I think the materialist account is not true. My goal in this section is to begin to explain why. To be clear, my goal is *not* to question the reasonableness of those who have a different viewpoint. Instead, I wish to highlight some of the considerations that have

[1]For a good introduction to the theories of mind, see J. Searle, *Mind: A Brief Introduction* (Oxford: Oxford University Press, 2005).

personally persuaded me. The considerations I am about to share changed my thinking in a dramatic way.

It all starts with a construction problem. We have seen in previous chapters that some constructions are impossible. For example, it is impossible to construct a purple floor from purely white tiles. It is impossible to construct prime ministers out of prime numbers. It is impossible to construct a self-sufficient totality from purely dependent things. And so on. These constructions all share the same problem: they commit a construction error.

A construction error results from building something with the wrong materials. White tiles, for example, are the wrong materials to build a purple floor. Numbers are the wrong materials for building a person. Similarly, as I will explain, I think molecules are the wrong materials for building a mind.

To get clearer about the nature of the problem, it will help to have a closer look at certain features of minds. I will focus on these three: (1) *qualia*, (2) *private access*, and (3) the *power to choose*. I will share why I think none of these features can flow from purely material features. Each presents a construction problem. Once the problem is fully in view, I will then propose a solution.

Qualia. Let's start with *qualia*. Qualia are the "feeling" aspects of sensations. An itchy sensation, for example, *feels* a certain way. This certain feeling is what philosophers call a *quale* (the singular of qualia).

Qualia are what make an emotion different from mere motion. When sawdust moves in the wind, the motion of the dust has no feeling to it. It has no quale.

Contrast qualia with the non-sense features of unconscious bits of matter, like dust. Dust has "third-person" characteristics, like these: shape, motion, mass, and so on. Third-person properties leave out *first-person properties* that characterize felt experiences. For example, a Starbucks cup has shape, but its shape is not the same as your first-person *experience* of its shape. Similarly, the motion of some molecules is not the same as your experience of seeing those molecules in motion. In general, the *experience* of mass, motion, and shape is not the same as mass, motion, or shape.

This difference between sense and non-sense inspires a question: if non-sense properties differ from first-person sense properties, how do first-person properties come into the world? Shifts in shapes lead to more shapes. So how do *sensations* come to be? Is it possible to construct sense from non-sense? How?

To help us think about this question, let us suppose we wanted to build a robot with genuinely first-person experiences. How would we do it? To be clear, I am not talking about merely getting a robot to *act* like it has feelings. We could build a robot that functions *as if* it has the experience of an itch: for example, it could exhibit the motions of an itchy person. Yet functioning *as if* it has a sensation is not the same as actually having sensations. A robot could scratch its leg without actually *feeling* anything. The robot is missing something: it is missing *sense.*

The hard problem here is to figure out how to build first-person sensations, in principle, out of purely non-sensing materials.

The challenge of building a person purely from non-sensing particles pierced my mind one morning as I woke up and saw a pattern of dust. The sun was shining through my window, and I saw dust bits glistening in the light. I stared at the motions of the dust. Then, in the flash of a thought, it occurred to me with crystal clarity that the motions of those dust bits do not make the dust *feel* anything. I considered the location of the dust. Location is irrelevant: dust could have any location on earth without feeling anything. The amount of dust also makes no difference. Then my mind made the obvious inference: *even dust that moves in the same pattern as the particles of my brain feels nothing.* I saw the construction problem clearly: purely third-person aspects—shapes, sizes, motions, masses, and so on—are insufficient materials for constructing the first-person "sense" aspects of a mind.

So how did sense come to exist? I will later consider the proposals that (1) sense does not exist, or (2) sense is actually the same as non-sense (from another perspective). For now, let us suppose sense exists and that sense has the sense-aspects *it seems to have* when you focus on your own sensations. How does this sense come to exist?

At this point, one might wonder whether qualia could somehow *emerge* from purely non-sense qualities. Consider, by comparison, the way certain properties of water, like liquidity and wetness, emerge from its molecular structure. While the atoms that make up water are not themselves liquid or wet, given a certain geometric arrangement, the H_2O structure *as a whole* is liquid and wet. The idea, then, is that while liquidity and wetness are irreducible properties, they emerge given the right conditions. Perhaps consciousness is like that: it just emerges under the certain conditions. Call this proposal "emergentism."

The emergentist proposal merits an entire book in its own right.[2] Here I shall attempt to explain succinctly why I don't think emergentism solves the problem. I have two points to make. First, the alleged cases of "emergence" are not like qualia, or they end up *smuggling in* qualia into the causes. Consider liquidity, for example. This property has a functional analysis in terms of water's molecular structure together with more basic physical laws. This functional analysis provides a way to reduce liquidity to other more basic properties. The *felt* aspect of consciousness, by contrast, is characteristically irreducible to non-felt qualities. So it isn't like liquidity.

Or take *wetness*. Although this property doesn't seem to be analyzable in terms of purely non-wet qualities, that's because wetness includes a qualitative feel, which is the very aspect of consciousness we are trying to explain. In general, for every candidate emergent property, it seems to me that either a reductive analysis is possible, or the property smuggles in the target phenomenon: felt consciousness. Thus, the problem remains unsolved.

Second, and more significantly, the term *emergentism* merely labels the mystery. It is not a solution. To illustrate, suppose you see water springing out of a rock. You might wonder, *How can water be coming out of that rock?* Here is one simple answer: the water *emerges* from the rock. That answer is not satisfying, however. Reflection on the nature of water reveals that water cannot come *solely from* the rock by itself. To make water out of a rock is to commit a construction error: a rock is the wrong kind of material for making water.

Sure, we may *say* the water "emerged" from the rock. But saying that solves nothing. We can still wonder how the water appears at that rock

[2]See, for example, W. Hasker, *The Emergent Self* (Ithaca, NY: Cornell University Press, 1999).

in the first place. Where did the *water* come from? This much is sure: the rock is not the whole story.

Private access. Here is another feature of your consciousness: your consciousness is directly knowable by you. You have *direct access* to what you are feeling.

Suppose you have an itch. That itch feels a certain way to you. How do you know how it feels? By awareness: when you focus on an itch, you are aware of how it feels to you. This awareness is your direct access to your itchy feeling.

A neuroscientist, by contrast, does not have *direct* conscious access to the feeling of your itches. When a scientist probes a brain, the scientist only has access to layers of gray matter (and even this access is mediated through the scientist's own *experiences*). By inspecting the aspects of gray matter, the scientist witnesses third-person aspects like mass, motion, and molecular structures. The scientist does *not* witness the first-person sense aspects of your itchy sensation.

To be clear, someone looking at a pattern of neurons in your brain might come to *believe* you are having an itchy feeling. But this belief arises from an *inference*, not by direct access. When a scientist sees molecules move, the scientist is not thereby seeing what it feels like to be you.

The two ways of accessing you reveal two sides of you: a public side and a private side. The public side includes publicly viewable aspects, like the shapes and motions of molecules. The private side, by contrast, includes those aspects that you alone access directly, like how you are feeling right now.

Going Deeper

We could theorize that you have just one side: your private side actually is your public side. When you access your private itchy feeling, for example, you are actually accessing molecules in your brain—just *from a first-person perspective*.

Something is right about this proposal. You can indeed view a single thing from different perspectives. For example, you can view a coin up close, and you can view a coin from far away. The coin you see is not the same as the way you see the coin.

However, let us not make the mistake of confusing the ways we see with the aspects we see. Suppose you and I look at a coin from different perspectives. I see heads, while you see tails. Then we have different perspectives on the same coin. Notice, however, that we are not seeing the exact same aspects of that coin. The one coin has two sides, after all. It would be a mistake, therefore, to say that the heads side is just the same as the tails side. Our different perspectives on the coin reveal different aspects of the one coin.

In the same way, different perspectives on you reveal different aspects of you. Your first-person perspective on your feelings reveals certain private, sense aspects of your feelings. It is true that these private aspects belong to the same person as any public aspects you may have. You are one being, after all. Yet, just as one coin has two sides, you have two sides—public and private.

I will say more soon about your power to see differences between private and public aspects. For now, I wish merely to highlight a connection between perspectives and properties: different perspectives can reveal different properties.

Part of the construction problem, then, is about constructing private aspects from purely public aspects. To see the problem clearly, suppose we want to construct a conscious statue from clay. Our ingredients are public: anyone can study the aspects of the clay we use. The statue we make is also public. A group of people could examine our statue and inspect its size, shape, structure, and so on. From public aspects of the clay, we get public aspects of the statue. How, then, can we construct the *private* aspects of consciousness?

Suppose we wish to install an itchy feeling that *only* the statue could be aware of. The problem is that we don't have the materials to do that: from public aspects (like shapes), we only get public aspects (more shapes). How could we ever construct the private *sense* side of the statue?

At this point, someone might wonder whether neuroscience has shown that we could give this statue an itchy feeling by moving around some shapes. After all, science reveals a *connection* between an itch and a neural network. Perhaps, then, we could give the statue an itchy feeling by installing a certain neural network.

I want to be very clear about the nature of the problem. The problem has a way of hiding under a cloak of familiar experience. It is part of familiar experience that physical events affect consciousness: knocking someone on the head will affect how they feel. One might wonder, then, what the deep problem is supposed to be. Is the problem supposed to be that brain activity *cannot* cause consciousness? But brain activity obviously does cause consciousness. What, then, is the problem?

The deep problem I am attempting to point to is about the *nature of the connection*. How does a neural network connect with an itch? To see a connection is not yet to have insight into what *makes* the connection possible. Even if a state X comes from state Y (like water springing from a rock), seeing this connection is not the same as seeing the source of that connection.

To illustrate further, suppose you see a lamp glowing after a flip of a switch. This sight does not yet reveal *how* the light switch makes the lamp glow. In the same way, you might glow with happiness after some chemicals interact. But the question remains: *how* do chemicals make the happy sensation? How does a change in motion cause a change in emotion? Seeing the connection doesn't explain the connection.

I'd like to share why I think the need for a deeper explanation is easy to miss. For some of you, this paragraph is going to remove the cloak. The cloak flows from the familiar. To illustrate what I mean, consider a cartoon show. In this show, the motions of the character's mouths synchronize with certain sounds. This synchronization is familiar. It is so familiar, in fact, that while you are engrossed in the show, you might be tempted to think the characters on the screen are literally *making* the sounds. The familiar connection cloaks the deeper explanation. On reflection, however, you can be sure the pixilated characters cannot be making the sounds. Pixels are insufficient materials.

In the same way, the deep problem of consciousness is about having sufficient materials for consciousness. We can see, by reason, that certain materials are insufficient. For example, we can see that prime numbers are insufficient materials for making a prime minister. Similarly, I think we can see, by reason, that purely third-person aspects are insufficient for making a first-person experience. If so, then the challenge is to see what materials *could* be sufficient. More on that later.

Free will. Stop reading this. Can you? Is it up to *you* whether you continue reading? If so, then you have some measure of "free will." In other words, you have the power to choose between options.

You might be unsure whether you actually have free will. Perhaps you are open to the idea that physical laws take away your free will. It is understandable: the particles in your brain follow the laws of physics, and the laws of physics are not up to you. In other words, if particles pull all the strings, then you are a puppet of their powers.

It is not my purpose here to force you to believe in free will (or anything else). My goal, rather, is to highlight an additional feature that you might think you have: *the power to choose.*

Here, briefly, is one reason you might think you have the power to choose. You *sense* yourself making choices. Consider this: senses are your windows into reality. Your visual sense of tables and chairs, for example, is your window into an actual world with tables and chairs. Your sense of your own thoughts is your window into actual thoughts within your mind. Similarly, your sense of your own power to make choices may be a window into your actual power to make choices.

While senses *can* mislead, they don't *have to*. Your sense that you are seeing words on a page *could* be an illusion. But it probably isn't. Unless you have some reason (presumably via some *sense*) to doubt your sense, your sense itself provides you with some evidence. So, if you do have the sense of yourself making choices, your sense of choice is some evidence for the reality of choice, just as your sense of these words is some evidence for the reality of these words.

Now if you do think you have at least some power to make choices, then you may appreciate an additional problem with building minds from mindless molecules. The problem is about constructing your power to choose. How do you build a power to choose from particles that have no power of their own to make any choices? Particles obey physical laws, and it is not up to *them* whether to obey those laws. All particles everywhere obey laws without any choice. Either the particles move deterministically along a single fixed path, or they move randomly. Either way, they make no choices. How, then, can *you* have the power to make choices?

How does choice arise from non-choice? Whatever one's answers to these questions, they invite a deeper look into the nature of minds.[3]

THE HARD PROBLEM

Let us take a step back and consider the root of these three problems we just considered. The root is that mere molecules are the wrong materials to build a mind. Molecules have third-person, public features, like shape, motion, and mass. Third-person, public features are insufficient to explain first-person, private features, like the feeling of an itch. How could you construct an emotion out of mere motions, a sensation from just shapes, or a person's private feelings purely from public aspects of particles? Philosophers call the problem of constructing the first-person sense from pure non-sense the *Hard Problem*.

Let us consider some proposed solutions to the Hard Problem. We may divide all solutions into three options. First option: deny that any minds exist. Second option: reduce minds to forms of matter. Third option: use additional resources beyond forms of matter. Let us consider each in turn.

Option 1: No minds. If there are no minds, then there are no thoughts, feelings, or beliefs. The Hard Problem is gone.[4] We don't need to explain the origin of minds because there are no minds.

This solution indicates the seriousness of the Hard Problem of consciousness. The problem of building sense from non-sense is so hard that some philosophers have proposed that the best solution is to deny that any conscious minds exist at all. I met a philosopher once who denied his own existence. After probing why, he said he didn't see how particles could produce people—*in principle*. "There are only particles," he explained, "therefore, there are no people."

While this solution does indeed remove the Hard Problem of consciousness, I do not recommend it. If consciousness were not real,

---

[3] I do not wish to give the impression that materialists have nothing to say about these questions. One idea is that choices are somehow *compatible* with a "bottom-up" (from particles to person) determinism. Rather than enter into particular theories of the nature of choices, my purpose is to draw attention to the kinds of questions that point to a more fundamental challenge, as I will describe next.

[4] See W. Ramsey, "Eliminative Materialism," *Stanford Encyclopedia of Philosophy* (2013), https://plato.stanford.edu/entries/materialism-eliminative/.

then there would be no thoughts, feelings, or emotions. Yet there are thoughts, feelings, and emotions. You have some. If you think you have no thoughts, then you have the *thought* that you have no thoughts. If you believe you have no beliefs, then you have the *belief* that you have no beliefs. If you feel that I am wrong in some of my beliefs, then you have a *feeling*. Although some philosophers have gone so far as to deny the existence of thoughts, feelings, and beliefs, their denial only reflects the seriousness of the Hard Problem.

I suspect you will agree that you have some thoughts, beliefs, and feelings. So, I will continue.

Option 2: Mind is "third-person" matter. A second proposal is to reduce first-person sense aspects to purely third-person, non-sense aspects of matter. For example, the sense of happiness *just is* some pattern of particles in your brain.[5] Could that be true?

The eminent philosopher of mind John Searle thinks reducing "sense" aspects of a mind to non-sense aspects of matter is actually just another way of denying the reality of consciousness. For Searle, to say "sense" is nothing but non-sensing materials is like saying a "car" is nothing but a carburetor, a "giraffe" is nothing but a telephone pole, or "understanding Chinese" is nothing but a Chinese grammar book. These reductions are actually eliminations.[6] In other words, to say mind is matter is just another way of saying there are no minds.

To see why Searle says this, consider the following aspects of mind and matter, respectively: (1) the sense of an itch and (2) being triangular. These aspects are different. Here is how you can tell: by your power of awareness. If you focus on an itch and then focus on a triangle, you can see some differences. You can see, for example, that an itchy feeling doesn't have three sides. Even if the itch occupies a region of your skin that takes the shape of a triangle, the *feeling* aspect of the itch is not the same as its triangular shape. The feeling is not a triangle. In fact, it is not any shape.

This power to see differences is the same power by which you can see that a triangle is different from a square. A square has four sides, while

[5]See S. Gozzano and C. Hill, *New Perspectives on Type Identity* (Cambridge: Cambridge University Press, 2012).
[6]Searle, *Mind*, 83-132.

a triangle has only three sides. You see that four is not three. How? By *direct awareness*.

You have direct awareness when you are directly aware of things. For example, you are directly aware of your thoughts. Think about a zebra. Did you? You can answer my question by being aware of whatever thought you just had. You do not need to check the molecular structure of your brain. Just focus on your thoughts. If you do, you are directly aware of them.

By focusing on your thoughts, you can be aware of their differences. Follow this procedure: first, focus on your thoughts; next, compare them; finally, notice their differences. You "notice" their differences by direct awareness. It is that easy.

Direct awareness gives you the power to see *some* things clearly. You can see clearly, for example, that a sad sensation is not the same as a happy sensation. You see this by focusing directly on these sensations within you. You can then see some of their differences. Again, you see their differences by direct awareness.

Direct awareness is a powerful tool. Without direct awareness, you would know nothing. You would not know that truth is different from falsehood. You would not know that *something* is different from *nothing*. You would not even know that you exist.

Going Deeper

Direct awareness works when you have direct awareness of things. For example, you have direct awareness of your thoughts and feelings. This direct awareness allows you to see—directly—differences between them.

In many cases, by contrast, you only have indirect awareness. For example, when you see a coin, you are aware of that coin by being aware of a side of that a coin (or your experience of that side). Indirect awareness is not as reliable as direct awareness. When Lois Lane sees Superman, she is not directly aware of Superman. She experiences an image of his face, his cape, and the way he talks. This experience is inside her, and she is aware of it directly. Superman, by contrast, is not wholly inside of her mind. For this reason, while her awareness of Superman's appearance is direct, her awareness of Superman is indirect. Her lack of *direct* awareness of Superman explains why she fails to realize that Superman is the same as Clark Kent. She is not directly aware of Superman. She is only directly aware of her experience of his attributes. By contrast, you have direct awareness of some aspects of your own thoughts and feelings. That is why you can be sure that a sad sensation differs from a happy sensation. You have direct awareness of some differences.

Incredibly, we can apply the power of direct awareness to test the hypothesis at hand. Recall the hypothesis: mental aspects are nothing but third-person aspects of matter. To illustrate, suppose that every aspect of a sensation is nothing but the form matter takes when neurons fire in a certain way. What is a "form of matter"? We can analyze forms in terms of third-person geometric properties. When neurons fire in a certain way, their "pattern" is a fancy shape in motion. So, can sense aspects *be* complex shapes in motion?

To answer this question, use your power of direct awareness: just as you can see that your sense of an itch is different from a triangle, you can use this same power to compare your sense of an itch with *any* complicated pattern of shapes, motions, networks, or function. Use the following procedure: focus on a sensation, compare its aspects with any geometric structure, and notice any differences.

To be clear, I am not saying that your sensations do not *connect* with forms of matter. On the contrary, I think shapes and sensations are connected: when brains change shape, certain sensations change. This connection is like the connection between a light switch and a glowing lamp: when the light switch changes position, the lamp glows. My point remains: just as the flipping of the switch differs from the glowing of the lamp, the motions of matter differ from the sensations I feel. It seems to me that I can see this difference *clearly* by direct awareness. I predict you can too.

Moreover, by direct awareness, I think we can see that the Hard Problem has nothing to do with the *number* or *complexity* of shapes. Happiness is not one triangle or *two*. Increasing the complexity of the shape makes no difference. The problem is that shapes are the wrong category. Just as prime numbers are the wrong materials for constructing a prime minister, shapes are the wrong materials for constructing the sense aspects of a sensation. Direct awareness into the nature of shapes reveals this.

In summary, some aspects of minds are more than third-person aspects of matter. For example, minds include first-person, privately accessed "sense" aspects. These sense aspects differ from non-sense aspects of matter. You can see these differences in the same way you can see that a triangle is not a square—by direct awareness.

Going Deeper

For the mathematically inclined, I wish to give the seed of another, independent way to see into the nature of consciousness. This way is through counting. I will unpack the reasoning in three steps. Step one: start with concepts. We can define unique concepts in terms of material states. Here is how. Take any conceivable material configuration, such as a snowflake or pile of leaves. A mental image of that particular configuration is then conceivable (i.e., consistent with necessary principles of reason). By this mental image, we can define a concept of that configuration. For example, there is the concept of a pile of leaves. When I say we can define a concept, I mean that the concept is conceivable—that is, without contradiction.

Step two: define thoughts out of *logical connections* between concepts. We can combine concepts to form thoughts. For example, there is the conceivable thought that a snowflake exists *or* that a pile of leaves exists. Since we have a conceivable concept for every conceivable material configuration, we can now define a thought for every *group* of conceivable material configurations.

Final step: apply Cantor's theorem. Georg Cantor showed us that groups outnumber individuals. More precisely, he showed that for any set (or plural) of things, there is a bigger set defined by the groups of its members. That's true even for infinite sets: there are more groups of members of an infinite set than individual members of that infinite set. By this result (which is Cantor's theorem), it follows from the previous two steps that there are more conceivable ways to *think* than there are conceivable ways to configure matter.[7] From here, it follows that the nature of thinking cannot be the same as the nature of matter. If they were the same, the number of conceivable ways to think couldn't be higher than the number of conceivable ways to configure matter. But it is.

This presentation is just a beginning.[8] Take what serves you; leave what does not. If my analysis is correct, one can have two eyes—the eye of direct awareness and the eye of counting—by which one can see the irreducibility of minds to material forms.

Option 3: More resources. I will now show how we can solve the Hard Problem with more resources. In particular, I will explain why I think *foundational* mentality supplies the resources to solve every aspect of the Hard Problem. Foundational mentality solves the three components of the construction problem: (1) qualia, (2) private access, and (3) free will.

First, if mentality exists at the foundational layer of reality, then this foundation could be the ultimate cause of the first-person "sense" that minds have. The foundation would itself include a first-person sense. Instead of shifting from pure non-sense to sense, sense exists at the foundation of things. Thus, the foundational mind could construct first-person properties from first-person sense properties. Sense materials are then the ultimate building materials for all sensations.

Second, the foundational mental layer would include the resources to produce minds that possess the power of private access. The foundational mind would have that same power. It would have the power to access its (or their) own thoughts and intentions directly. Thus, the

[7]You might wonder whether we could reverse the argument: for example, can arbitrary configurations of matter combine to form larger material states? My answer is that reversing the argument generates inconsistencies, such as the inconsistency of combining a leaf with an object that is maximally dense and occupies all possible space. By contrast, no inconsistency arises from conjoining *thoughts* about arbitrary materials.

[8]I develop this argument in Rasmussen, "Building Thoughts from Dust: A Cantorian Puzzle," *Synthese* 192 (2015): 393-404; and "Against Non-Reductive Physicalism," in *The Blackwell Companion to Substance Dualism*, ed. Jonathan J. Loose, Angus J. L. Menuge, and J. P. Moreland, (Malden, MA: Wiley-Blackwell, 2018), 328-39.

foundational mental reality could create other minds that have the power of direct access to their own thoughts and intentions.

Third, foundational mentality would include the resources to build beings that have the power to make choices. Here is how. Suppose the foundation forms laws of motion that leave some options open for other minds. As physicists tell us, not all physical laws are completely *deterministic*: a particle may go one way *or* another. Particles leave options open. With some options open, the foundation could then intentionally form beings with the power to make choices *within* some of the open options. In this case, particles do not completely pull people along. Power can flow the other way: people have the power to pull particles along within the open options.

To illustrate, you have the power to choose whether to focus on these words or to release your focus. This power is within the options available to you, at least *if* it is within the options available to the particles. Choose your focus, and particles in your brain will *thereby* take a path. (Recent science of the mind-brain connection supports this result.[9])

Fundamental mentality, therefore, can solve the problem of consciousness by providing the resources to construct the three aspects of conscious minds we considered. This solution flips mind and matter. Mind is primary. Matter comes from mind. (I will discuss how matter could come from mind in the next chapter.)

Without any foundational mentality, by contrast, the building materials are fundamentally different. There are then no sensations to build sensations, no power of private access to produce your powers of private access, and no powers of choice to produce your power to stop reading.

The thoughts I am attempting to release to you are just a beginning. Each aspect of consciousness is like a crack in the materialist framework. In my experience, inspecting these cracks does not make them go away. Quite the opposite: the closer you inspect aspects of your own consciousness, the more power you have to see holes in materialism's structural integrity.

I offer a final note about the origin of the Hard Problem. The Hard Problem is not a Sunday school invention designed to knock down

---

[9]See M. Beauregard and D. O'Leary, *The Spiritual Brain: A Neuroscientist's Case for the Existence of the Soul* (San Francisco: HarperOne, 2008).

skeptics. No pastor or priest discovered the problem. *Materialist philosophers* did. They spearheaded the discussion of the problem. In fact, the person who coined the term is a secular philosopher, David Chalmers.[10] Chalmers discovered the problem after reflecting on the first-person "sense" aspects of consciousness. He points out that consciousness cannot merely reflect a certain material complexity. Upon inspection, complexity is not enough; consciousness requires the right *category*. The Hard Problem arose, then, in the academic halls of philosophy, as philosophers pondered how to construct the sense side of people from purely non-sense materials.

In graduate school, I was intrigued to discover many professional, materialist philosophers who responded to the Hard Problem by eliminating the "sense" aspects of minds altogether. They say we have no thoughts, beliefs, or sensations.[11]

Fortunately, we do not need to think there are no thoughts. Instead, we can follow Chalmers. Chalmers's solution is that the foundation of things includes what he calls *proto-consciousness*. Proto-consciousness has the same categorical nature as the consciousness we experience. Whether we call the foundational mind "proto-conscious" or just "conscious," the point is the same: a mind-like foundation provides the materials to construct all other mental aspects of reality, including yours.

SUMMARY

The foundation of existence is the foundation of conscious minds. *How*?

We need the right materials. Suppose the foundation only has "public" properties, like mass, shape, or motion. Then we have a construction problem. The problem is about building private, sense properties purely from public, non-sense properties alone. How is that possible? The third-person aspects of molecules only combine to form more complex, third-person aspects—shapes on shapes.

---

[10] D. Chalmers, "Facing Up to the Problem of Consciousness," *Journal of Consciousness Studies* 2, no. 3 (1995): 200-219.

[11] Examples include Patricia Churchland, *Neurophilosophy: Toward a Unified Science of the Mind/Brain* (Cambridge, MA: MIT Press, 1986); Paul Churchland, *A Neurocomputational Perspective* (Cambridge, MA: MIT Press, 1989); and S. Stitch, *Deconstructing the Mind* (New York: Oxford University Press, 1996).

Both reason and experience testify that complex shapes are still shapes. Public properties are public properties no matter how complex. Public properties don't add up to private properties. Non-sense properties never add up to sense. How, then, can any private sense properties ever belong to anything?

We can solve the construction problem with "mental" materials, such as sensations, thoughts, and intentions. With these materials at the ultimate foundation, it is possible to construct the first-person, private properties of a mind.

CHAPTER 8

FOUNDATION OF MATTER

HOW TO MAKE A UNIVERSE

A few years ago, I wanted to make a computer program that would simulate a universe. My goal was ambitious: I wanted to make the universe suited for a randomized evolution of complex bodies. This project was part of Templeton's 2013–2015 Randomness and Divine Providence Project. My assignment was to create a program that could produce digital creatures using random processes.

The project was hard. How do you simulate a universe that produces complex creatures? To get started, I had to answer many questions. What are the building blocks of my universe? How many blocks are there? What are their properties? How do they move? How do they interact? Since I wanted to create complex creatures, I also had to figure out how the blocks could combine to form complex blocks. I had to figure out how the creatures could live, die, and multiply. It became obvious that in order to simulate a universe with creatures, I needed to set up many things.

Part of the challenge of my project was to figure out which starting points *could* lead to anything interesting. To get a universe with creatures in it, I needed to have some "materials" that could form into creatures. I needed building blocks. I also needed rules to define the features of the building blocks, including their size, length of existence, manner of motion, and so on. Plus, I needed to have rules that allowed the blocks to interact. A simple rule of attraction produced nothing but a static blob, while a simple rule of repelling produced nothing but scattering dots—forever.

To get stable building blocks for creatures—ever—required lots of forethought.

To illustrate the fine-tuning required, imagine that the basic parameters of my toy universe are dials. Different settings on the dials define different universes. For example, let us say that one of the dials governs the number of basic (indivisible) blocks—the "atoms." This number could be set to 0, 1, 2, 3, 4, and so on. If the number of atoms is set to 0, then the universe is blank. If it is set to 1, then the universe has a single, lonely atom. A different dial governs how atoms interact. For example, when we set the dial to a certain setting, all atoms repel in a perfectly symmetrical way. The setting on the dial indicates how strongly the atoms repel each other. So, if the dial is 0, then everything is stationary. If the dial is 1, perhaps that means things move apart the length of one atom per second. If the dial is -1, then they move together.

By reason alone, we can see that specific conditions are required for life to exist in any conceivable universe, whether digital or material, that contains complex lifeforms. For example, by reason, we can see that a universe with *nothing in it* will be an empty canvas, forever. By reason, we can see that a universe with things that only repel each other will produce an endless scatter, with no complex unities anywhere, ever. By reason, we can see that a universe with things that only attract each other will only form a blob, forever. And so on. Any universe with organized complexity depends on specific parameters. Random dials set to random settings don't automatically produce a life-suitable universe. My computer simulation made this point obvious.

Recent science is a second witness to the fine-tuning requirement. In the last several decades, physicists have been able to measure with increasing accuracy what it takes for a universe like ours to be suitable for any stability at all. For example, one feature of the universe is its *rate of expansion* (determined by the so-called "cosmological constant"). This rate is like a dial that requires a very precise value for any stable organization. Physicists tell us that if you turn this dial slightly to the right, then matter and anti-matter completely annihilate each other, and the universe collapses into nothing. If you turn it slightly to the left, then the universe expands too quickly to form anything but scattering hydrogen and helium atoms.

Physicist Alan Lightman summarizes these observations as follows: "If these fundamental parameters were much different from what they are, it is not only human beings who would not exist. No life of any kind would exist."[1]

Science joins with reason, then, to testify that the dials for a stable universe must have precise settings. Fine-tuning expert Robin Collins offers an illustration to indicate the degree of precision. Getting a universe with life in it is like hitting a one-inch target, he estimates, by launching a dart across the entire Milky Way.[2] Such a launch would need to be extremely calculated and precisely executed to succeed in hitting the target. Collins calculates that the dials that define the basic features of our universe need to be at least as precise for any lifeforms to come on the scene anywhere, ever.

In view of the fine-tuning conditions, one may wonder why our universe has produced lifeforms. Although the existence of lifeforms is familiar, their existence is far from trivial. The degree of precision required for a universe to have lifeforms invites a question: Why is any universe suited for lifeforms?

This question takes us back to the foundation of things. The foundation of all existence is the foundation of everything in existence, including mind and matter. To see how a foundation *could* be the foundation for the organization of matter, I will assess the main proposals on offer. Then I will show how the account of the foundation given in the previous chapter predicts precisely the right resources to explain the existence of a universe suitable for lifeforms.

HOW TO EXPLAIN ORGANIZED MATTER

Proposal 1: Chance. Improbable things happen. For example, people win the lottery. The explanation is chance. Similarly, perhaps the explanation of a fine-tuned universe is just chance. No deeper explanation exists.

Analysis. Is chance the *best* explanation? Consider that the words on this page exist. One explanation of their existence is chance: I randomly

[1]A. Lightman, "The Accidental Universe," *Harper's*, December 2011, https://harpers.org/archive/2011/12/the-accidental-universe/.

[2]R. Collins, "God, Design, and Fine-Tuning," in *God Matters: Readings in the Philosophy of Religion*, ed. R. M. Bernard, 54-65 (London: Longman, 2003).

typed letters, or they randomly appeared from nowhere. According to this chance explanation, the letters formed meaningful sentences *just by chance*. This explanation may be conceivable, but it is highly improbable.

Or suppose Suzy's dad is in charge of a lottery. Suzy wins the lottery ten times in a row. In this case, the chance hypothesis is suspect. It is improbable that Suzy wins by chance. The hypothesis that Suzy's dad rigs the election is far more probable.

Why isn't chance the best explanation in these cases? Here is why: a *better* explanation is available. While it is possible that Suzy won the lottery ten times by chance, it is more probable that her dad had a hand in it. Similarly, while it is possible these words appeared by chance, it is more probable that they came from some mind.

Suppose we appeal to chance to explain the universe. Then we fall into an abyss of improbability. The dials of the universe must be within narrow ranges for life to emerge. While it is possible that Collins's arrow travelled across the Milky Way to hit a one-inch target, it is *improbable* by chance.

If we must fall into the abyss of improbability, then so be it. Yet, another explanation is available. We have already seen that a *mental* foundation would have the resources to construct other minds. A mental foundation would also have the resources to set the dials of our universe, as I will explain further under Proposal 7. If that is right, then we do not need to fall into the abyss of improbability.

In summary, chance creates a probability problem. Just as these very words you see are improbable by mere chance, so too the conditions for life are improbable by mere chance. Moreover, just as these words are more likely to exist if there is a mind behind them, so too matter is more likely to allow for the existence of lifeforms if there is a mind behind matter. (I will say something about how a mind *could* be behind matter under Proposal 7.)

Proposal 2: Because you exist. The reason the universe is suited for your existence is simple: it had to be for *you* to consider the question. After all, you cannot discover that a universe is *not* suited for your existence. If the universe were not suited for your existence, you wouldn't observe anything. You wouldn't exist. Thus, your existence explains why the universe is suited for your existence.

Analysis. The objection gets *something* right, but it doesn't get to the root of things. To illustrate what I mean, I'll tell you a story. You are about to be executed. Suddenly poison gases start pouring into your room. You fall asleep. The next morning you wake up, *alive*! In this story, the conditions for your survival were in place somehow. But how? Here is one answer: the conditions for your survival were in place *because you survived*. This "you survived" answer is obviously missing something, however. Surviving does not explain why or how you survived. It is true that if the conditions were not suited for your survival, you would not survive. Nevertheless, your survival does not explain why the conditions were in place for your survival.

In the same way, the "you exist" explanation is incomplete. True, if the universe were not suited for life, you would not exist. Nevertheless, your existence does not explain why the conditions were in place for your existence in the first place. Why does any life-suitable universe exist at all?

Here, perhaps, is why some people give the "you exist" explanation. Here is what is right about it: we could not *find out* about a fine-tuned universe if we had not existed. In some sense, then, our existence helps explain the fact that we could *find out* the conditions required for us to exist. That much is right.

By seeing what is right about the "exist explanation," we can see why something is still missing. An explanation of why you found something out is different from an explanation of the thing you found out. Suppose you *find out* you survived a plot to kill you. Your survival doesn't explain how or why you survived. Similarly, the "you exist" explanation of fine-tuning does nothing to explain how or why the universe is suited for any lifeforms. While it may be inevitable that *if* advanced lifeforms exist, those lifeforms will discover that the universe is suited for their existence, it is not inevitable, by chance, that any universe with lifeforms exist. What remains to be explained is why the dials happen to be set to the life-permitting range.

Proposal 3: Deeper physics. We can explain the dials by deeper physical laws. While we may not yet know what the deeper physics is, we can hypothesize that some basic physical features determine that the dials will be set to the life-permitting range.

Analysis. This "deeper physics" answer, like the "you exist" explanation, is incomplete. It pushes the mystery back a step. What explains the deeper physics? Why does *the deepest physics* happen to give rise to the precise dial settings required for organized complexity?

Calling features "basic" only relabels the mystery. Suppose astronomers discover a star constellation that forms the following words: "The foundation of the universe caused these stars to exist." We might wonder why or how those stars managed to be arranged like *that.* Why would these stars just happen to form a meaningful sentence in English? Now suppose someone gives the following hypothesis: the star arrangement is an inevitable consequence of the most basic features of reality. This hypothesis doesn't remove the mystery. It only relabels it. Why would reality have features that happen to give rise to a *message* in the stars? Calling them "basic" does nothing to answer this deeper question.

Going Deeper

We can understand the *probability* that some features are basic in terms of *degree of expectation.* To illustrate, consider these very words on this page. Where did they come from? Here is one hypothesis: some necessary, basic rules of reality determines that these words appear without any intentional, mental activities. This "no-mind" hypothesis is improbable, however. It is improbable because it is unexpected that words like these would exist in the absence of mental activity. The hypothesis that the basic rules of reality lead to these words without any mental involvement is contrary to ordinary expectations. By contrast, words like these are just what you might expect from a mind. For this reason, the existence of these words is evidence of a mind behind them. You have evidence that the full explanation of the existence of this page of words is not merely a consequence of basic laws without any mind.

Proposal 4: Anything natural. The foundational mind theory is not a scientific theory. In fact, positing a mind behind matter is a science-stopper because this stops us from looking for naturalistic explanations.

While we may never know the full naturalistic explanation, it is better to be humble and honest enough to simply admit we just *don't know* the explanation.

Analysis. Humility and honesty will indeed protect us from error. Let us think carefully, then, about whether a foundational mind theory stops science.

First, it is possible to have evidence for the works of a mind. Consider, for example, these words you see here. Are they not evidence of a mind behind them?

In principle, we can even have evidence of non-human minds. Suppose we discover some caves on Mars. To our great astonishment, we discover something special inside these caves: we see neatly carved symbols depicting mountains and trees on the walls. Would science stop us from hypothesizing a mind behind these carvings? Would a mind hypothesis stop science?

Perhaps the real worry is not with minds per se but with the idea of a "supernatural" mind beyond all material forms. The worry here is that science reveals *natural* causes, not *supernatural* ones.

As I indicated in a previous chapter, I want to avoid stumbling over words. The words *natural* and *supernatural* have imprecise meanings that vary from person to person. My project is not to show you that any mind is beyond *all that we know*. Rather, I seek to explain how a mind could anchor the things we know. Rather than stumble over words, I propose we work with other words instead.

Here is a proposal for how a foundational mind could organize things in ways conducive to science. First, a foundational mind could have a *rational* nature. Its rationality is a feature by which the foundation "acts" in orderly, law-like ways. Discoveries of laws, then, would be discoveries of the order of the foundational mind. A foundational mind could cause motions and material organizations according to rational and discoverable patterns. For example, a foundational mind could cause symmetries of the early universe to break in precise ways to allow stars and planets to form. It could guide things to specific places in orderly, predictable, law-like ways.

We might call the foundational mind hypothesis *meta*-scientific, since it can explain the success of science itself. This ultimate mind would underlie the rational causal order. We could expect, on this account, that the foundational mind creates an order for other minds to investigate and discover layer by layer. Some patterns could be easy for us to understand, while others could beckon the cooperation of our best minds in an ongoing journey of discovery. Instead of blocking science, a foundational, rational mind could make science possible.

Proposal 5: Anything simple. Richard Dawkins raises an interesting and important objection to the foundational mind theory. He wonders what would explain the complexity of a cosmic designer. If complexity requires an explanation, then so does the complexity of a foundational mind. But that contradicts the fact that a *foundational* mind cannot have a designer.[3]

By Dawkins's lights, we do not need to be agnostic about whether there is design at the bottom of reality. We can be reasonably sure that a mind is *not* foundational because we can be reasonably sure that the foundation is not complex in the way a mind would be. Simple particles and laws are more probable than a complex mind.

Analysis. I appreciate Dawkins's point. In fact, it helps us. It shines light on our previous steps. Recall the step installed in chapter six. There I gave three independent tools to see that the foundation is simple ("purely actual"), like a tree trunk from which all complex branches, leaves, and fruit spring forth. These tools support Dawkins's point: the foundation's basic nature lacks unnecessary complexity. I think Dawkins is right, then, that the most probable account of the foundation is the simplest. He is also right that you run into trouble if you try to explain all complexity in terms of even greater complexity. His points are good.

I agree with Dawkins, then: the most probable theory of the foundation is the simplest. (No "but" is coming!) It is unsurprising, in fact, that from ancient times to the present, people have theorized that the foundation has a simple description. This "simplicity" theory is indeed the most probable.

The only thing I wish to *add* is why Dawkins's preference for simplicity fits well with the foundational mind hypothesis we developed in

[3]R. Dawkins, *The God Delusion* (New York: Houghton Mifflin, 2006), 113.

the previous chapter. While simplicity may indeed cut against the theory that the foundation is a purely "third-person" *brain*, simplicity does not cut against a theory of a purely first-person substance.

In fact, Dawkins sharpens our theory. Here is how. To begin, I invite you to consider *yourself* from your first-person perspective. By focusing inwardly on yourself, you witness something familiar: *you*. Notice that your sense of *yourself* is not the same as your sense of your particular body. After all, you can sense yourself while you are dreaming, even while you lack any sense of your body on your bed. Your sense of *you* does not include a complex array of material forms. For this reason, the concept of a *first-person self* does not build in material complexity.

We can now apply this concept of a first-person self to the foundation. We could theorize that the foundation is a *purely* first-person self. Unlike your first-person self, which has connections with material forms, the foundational self could exist prior to all material forms.

This mind could then have thoughts in the most fundamental way. The fundamental mind does not first create a "law" that connects *its* thoughts with patterns of neurons. Rather, it thinks in a basic way. The inner nature of this fundamental mind would be pure, simple, and complete (i.e., purely actual).

This account is not complete. We may still wonder, for example, *how* a fundamental mind could exist prior to matter. I will say more about how a foundational mind could be foundational to everything else in the course of the next few chapters. We have more pieces to install.

For now, my primary aim is to highlight the advantage of Dawkins's insight. His insight points us to a simple theory of the foundation. The theory that the foundation has mental resources is not complex or ad hoc. It does not contradict anything we know. Instead, a foundational mind provides a deep explanation of the fine-tuning of material forms.[4] Thus, instead of posing an insurmountable problem for the foundational

[4]In fact, from what I can tell, developments in neuroscience point to foundational features of our *own* first-person mental. J. M. Schwartz and S. Begley, *The Mind and the Brain: Neuroplasticity and the Power of Mental Force* (New York: Harper Collins, 2002). Moreover, my Cantorian argument (J. Rasmussen, "Against Non-Reductive Physicalism," in *The Blackwell Companion to Substance Dualism*, ed. Jonathan J. Loose, Angus J. L. Menuge, and J. P. Moreland, 328–39 [Malden, MA: Wiley-Blackwell, 2018]) independently calls into question any *essential* dependence of person-mental episodes and material forms.

mind theory, Dawkins's insight sharpens our understanding of the foundation. The foundation could be a purely first-person mind without arbitrary limits or unnecessary complexities.

Proposal 6: Many universes. Maybe there are many, many universes—perhaps infinitely many. Then, some life-permitting universe will probably exist by chance.[5]

Analysis. The first thing to notice is that the many universe hypothesis does not *compete* with the foundational mind hypothesis. An ultimate mind could produce many universes. Even if many universes spring into being, they could *all* be the manifestation of a fundamental mind.

Second, and significantly, the mere multiplication of universes does not itself explain how even *one* universe could have lifeforms. Consider that an infinite number of car factories will never produce a turtle. Similarly, an infinite number of universes does not automatically guarantee that *any* universe is suited for life. All universes could be blobs of different sizes with no lifeforms.

At one time in my life, I imagined that perhaps we could explain the existence of life with the following hypothesis: all conceivable universes exist. This hypothesis is both simple and powerful. It predicts that we exist, since we are conceivable.

Upon further reflection, however, I discovered a problem. I noticed that some conceivable universes contradict other conceivable universes. For example, I can conceive of a universe with a black hole that spans the entire blob of everything. I can also conceive of a universe that is not inside a black hole. But I cannot conceive of both universes being real: there cannot be a black hole that spans everything and does not span everything. My simple hypothesis was too simple. Too bad![6]

---

[5]See, for example, M. Tegmark, *Our Mathematical Universe: My Quest for the Ultimate Nature of Reality* (New York: Random House, 2014) for a detailed development of the multiverse hypothesis.

[6]A similar problem afflicts the related hypothesis that all possible *geometries* exist. Some geometries exclude each other: for example, a maximally dense geometry that spans all possible dimensions and sizes excludes all other geometries. Another, independent problem is about explaining things *at particular regions*. For example, you can ask what best explains these words here in this note. One hypothesis is that these words have a completely mindless explanation, while another hypothesis is that some mind was behind these words. You might think the mind hypothesis is more likely, *irrespective* of the number of universes. This thought generalizes: for any given region of reality (for any universe or any part of any universe), the probability that a mind is behind things in *that* region is independent of the number of regions there happens to be. For a development of this argument (and a response to the "selection-effect" objection),

I eventually realized that even a multiverse would have dials. When I created my computer program to simulate a universe with life, I could make rules to define many "universes." Making such rules is not a shortcut, though, to making a program that simulates lifeforms. I still need a highly specified set of rules. Random rules don't work. For example, the rule that the universes attract its atoms at varying strengths only produces a multiverse with collapsing blobs. And the code for "let there be all conceivable rules" only entails a contradiction.

The problem is not with the limits of computing power but with the limits of reason. Without an ultimate mind, there is no mechanism—no reason—at the foundation to explain why any universe is ever suited for life.

Proposal 7: Intention. The foundational mind has the power to form intentions. Just as you could intentionally *aim* to set the dials on an alarm clock, a foundational mind could aim to set the dials of our universe.

Analysis. Let us take a step back and consider how to decide between hypotheses in general. Reason helps us. Suppose we have two hypothesis, H1 and H2, and we have some data D. Next, suppose that D fits better with H1 than with H2. That is, D is more *likely*—more *expected*—on H1 than on H2. Then, by reason, D is evidence for H1 over H2.

To illustrate, consider the words printed on this page. What explains their existence? Here is one hypothesis: there was random typing. Here is a different hypothesis: there was a mind with a goal to write something meaningful for you. Random typing is far less likely to produce meaningful sentences on a page than a mind. It follows, by reason, that the existence of these words is more likely if there is a mind behind them than if I randomly typed them.

We can apply the same "probability" reasoning to hypotheses about the foundation. Our data, D, is this: matter has organized into complex creatures. What explains D? We have two hypotheses on the table. H1 is the hypothesis that the foundation has the power to form intentions. H2 is the hypothesis that the foundation has no such power.

The foundational mind hypothesis has advantages. As we saw in the previous section, a mental foundation solves the Hard Problem

---

see M. Rota, *Taking Pascal's Wager: Faith, Evidence, and the Abundant Life* (Downers Grove, IL: InterVarsity Press, 2016), chap. 8.

of consciousness, for it provides construction materials for sensations, private access, and personal control. We can now see that a foundational mind provides an additional resource: a foundational mind would have the power to aim to organize matter into a place for embodied minds.

Moreover, a foundational mind, like other minds we know, would have reason within its nature to be interested in complexities, symmetries, and beauty of various kinds. Embodied minds exhibit complexities, symmetries, and beauty of various kinds. Therefore, a foundational mind would have some reason to form a universe that can allow for embodied minds.

Without a foundational mind, by contrast, the power to set the dials on purpose is missing from the foundation. In that case, nothing aims to organize matter into anything but a blob or a scatter of dots. In view of the many dials of fine-tuning, it is unexpected that the dials would all happen to be set for life. Getting matter to form complex creatures ever, anywhere, is like getting words on this page to form a meaningful sentence. With chance alone, it is unexpected.

Let me express these results humbly. Different people may estimate the probabilities differently, depending on everything they have considered. Here is my own estimate. It seems to me, by reason, that the existence of a universe in which the words on this page can arise (ever, anywhere) is more likely—unimaginably more likely—if a foundational mind underlies the organization of material forms than if the foundation is entirely mindless.

Going Deeper

You might wonder how a foundational mind could form matter's geometric forms. Here is one idea: the foundational mind has the same kind of power you have to form images in your own mind. When you close your eyes, you can see faint images. With some effort, you can cause these images to take certain forms. For example, you may be able to cause an image of a purplish box to appear in your mind. This image arises within the canvas of your imagination.

While your canvas is private to you, my hypothesis is that the foundational mind's canvas is public. This mind forms material objects with its power of imagination. In this way, the ultimate mind causes material objects to appear—rationally and orderly—on the public canvas we call "the universe."

I call this theory "The Imagination Theory" because it explains material forms in terms of the imagination of the foundation. The Imagination Theory is just one hypothesis. Take it or leave it.

HOW TO FINE TUNE EVOLUTION

When I created the computer program to simulate a universe, I wanted to do more than make a universe that *could* simulate complex creatures. I wanted to see actual creaturely shapes emerge on my computer screen.

So I did what you might expect: I programmed principles of evolution into my universe. First, I hard-coded some initial, simple lifeforms made from basic blocks. Second, I created rules by which the lifeforms could replicate. Through replication, the lifeforms could then produce more advanced versions of themselves. Then, I setup an environment in which natural selection could take over. Theoretically, the simpler creatures would then die off, leaving the more advanced versions to continue replicating. The goal was to observe what would happen to the surviving creatures over time.

Here is what I saw. Once I got my computer program up and running, I observed what happened in the different versions of the universe. For example, one version of my universe favored *longer* creatures (i.e., longer lines of connected blocks). Over time, the creatures evolved to produce increasingly long offspring. A different version favored *shorter* creatures. Over time, all those creatures reduced to the shortest possible length. In all my versions, I let the program run through many generations very quickly.

My program helped me verify two things. First, natural selection is a powerful way to reach a specified target. For example, when I wanted the creatures to decrease in length, I designed the environment to make longer creatures more susceptible to dying. Then I watched creatures "naturally" evolve into the shortest forms.

The second thing I verified is that natural selection by itself does not prefer complexity. To test the powers of natural selection, I created a version of my universe where the "target" of evolution was itself randomized. I randomized the target by randomizing the environment's rules by which creatures die and survive. I came up with three hypothesis to predict what I might find:

Hypothesis 1—From Simple to Complex: simple creatures randomly evolve to become more complex over time.

Hypothesis 2—Neutral: the maximum complexity of any organism in the environment stays about the same over time.

Hypothesis 3—From Complex to Simple: complex creatures randomly evolve to become simpler over time.

I then tested the hypotheses by observing the evolution of my creatures. I saw a consistent but surprising pattern: the creatures that initially had the most complexity (measured in terms of the number and arrangement of their parts) died off over time, leaving the simplest versions to continue the evolution. That result intrigued me. Many people have speculated that the "From Simple to Complex" hypothesis is true. My experiments disconfirmed that hypothesis. Instead, natural selection in a randomized complex adaptive system tended to prefer *simpler* creatures. In short, adaptation led to simplicity, not complexity.

I am not the only one to observe results like mine. The complexity research at the Santa Fe Research Institute is consistent with my findings.[7] Even their most "finely-tuned" evolution simulations have never produced anything as remotely sophisticated as a strand of DNA—let alone beings with the technological capacity to self-repair, mate, and design their own computers. While evolution can produce great complexity given the right setup, the complexity produced is a direct consequence of extremely precisely set dials. It is never random.

Here, then, is the data we have: while we can design fascinating evolution simulations, these same simulations reveal that evolution of complex creatures depends on many highly specific parameters. Contrary to popular opinion, the existence of biological evolution does not undermine design.

---

[7]For more on this subject, see, for example, A. Wagner, *Solving Evolution's Greatest Puzzle* (New York: Penguin, 2014).

It is the opposite. The very existence of an evolution in which turtles, giraffes, and humans can emerge reinforces the degree of fine-tuning of matter itself. The evolution of matter into creatures does not *explain* fine-tuning; it *depends on* it. Without a precise setup, no stable matter would exist, and hence no matter could even begin to evolve into anything.

I offer a final note about the existence of complex creatures on our planet. Scientists have discovered something remarkable about the creatures. Every one of them has DNA. This DNA is a common code that unites every complex creature on earth. Unfortunately, a firestorm of popular-level debates about "creation" vs. "evolution" often obscures a certain significant implication of this common code.

Consider what the common code implies. It implies that all complex creatures are "leaves" on a single tree with a single root. In other words, the dust of the earth didn't spawn many roots on different continents at different times. If dust did produce many complex creatures from different roots, there would be many trees of life. New, unrelated beings would emerge in random places at random times. As far as we observe, that never happens. If you kick some dust, you will not spawn a new evolution from scratch. New lifeforms don't get up and running nearly so easily.

The unity of the species, then, does nothing to undermine the fine-tuning. The opposite is so: biological unity confirms that getting life from non-life depends on exquisitely fine-tuned conditions. Everything in science—from the fine-tuning of the universe, to computer simulations, to genetic studies—points to this universal observation. The unity of the species further highlights the incredible fine-tuning of the material world.

SUMMARY

We have investigated the origin of two sides of you: your private mental side and your public material side. In the previous chapter, we saw how a mental foundation could provide useful construction materials—sensations, thoughts, and intentions. With these materials at the foundation, it is possible to construct the first-person, private, "sense" properties of other minds. In this chapter, we considered how to construct the material, public side of you.

Reason and science together testify that many dials will need to be within precise parameters in order for matter to take a stable, organized form anywhere, ever. We may wonder, then, why matter takes any stable, organized form. We considered several proposed explanations—for instance, basic physical laws, many universes, and so on. Yet without a foundational mind, all of these explanations merely move the bump under the carpet. Those very explanations require improbable, fine-tuned features.

By contrast, a foundational, purely actual, *first-person* foundation has a simplicity that does not depend on improbable fine-tuned constraints. After all, a foundational mind is describable in a non-arbitrary, theory-simple way. Moreover, a foundational mind would have reasons to produce something as interesting as a universe (or universes) suited for organized complexity. An ultimate mind within the foundation, then, makes good sense of why anything like you would ever exist.

CHAPTER 9

FOUNDATION OF MORALS

We are now ready to add the next step. This step is about the foundation of *right* versus *wrong*. I will install this step in three pieces. First, I will describe a tool by which we sense right and wrong. Second, I will propose how we may use this tool to investigate what Sam Harris calls "the moral landscape."[1] Third, I will seek an understanding of the *foundation* of both the moral landscape and your moral tool.

SENSING GOODNESS

Moral experience. As a person, you are capable of experiencing more than just thoughts and feelings. You can also experience *good* and *bad*, *right* and *wrong*, *better* and *worse*, *positive* and *negative*. For example, you can experience a good feeling when you treat someone kindly.

Good feelings are a clue about the kind of world we live in. It is easy to take for granted the sensation of good. The sense of good is familiar, but it is not insignificant.

Why do any experiences feel "good"? We can easily imagine a world without any good experiences. We can imagine, for example, organisms that can feel *cold* but that cannot feel *good*. Our world, incredibly enough, includes the feeling of good. The *feeling of good* is part of our world. Why?

---

[1]S. Harris, *The Moral Landscape: How Science Can Determine Human Values* (New York: Free Press, 2011).

The feeling of good is part of a larger dimension of reality, which we may call "moral experiences." Moral experiences includes all experiences of good, bad, right, wrong, positive, or negative. You may sense, for example, that rationality is good, while irrationality is not. Similarly, you may sense that false-seeking is worse than truth-seeking, or that intellectual dishonesty is not as noble as truth-telling. In general, you have many sensations that you can sort into *positive* and *negative*, *good* and *bad*. Call these sensations "moral sense."

Does your moral sense tell you anything about the world? If so, how?

Here is my proposal: your moral senses are a *window* into a moral landscape. For example, your sense of good, bad, right, and wrong help you see *something* about what is good and bad, right and wrong.

To be clear, your moral window, like any window, can have cracks, which can cause misperceptions. I am not suggesting that your moral window provides you with perfect sight. Rather, my proposal is that your moral window provides *some* sight to *some* extent.

Consider, on the other hand, a different proposal: moral senses are not windows. On this proposal, the sense that killing kids for fun is inappropriate is not a window into anything inappropriate. Nothing is actually inappropriate. Instead, our sense of wrongness indicates nothing but our own sense. Senses, on this account, may be merely personal preferences, evolved within us to help us survive.

So, which proposal is true? Do we have any reason to think our moral sense is a window? Do we have any reason to think moral sense reveals anything beyond the sense itself?

To begin to address this question, I will proceed as follows. First, I will offer an account of the nature of moral senses. Second, I will show how the account makes good sense of our moral language and moral actions. Third, I will respond to five objections that pose common barriers to the reliability of moral senses. My purpose is to remove barriers that may block you from seeing out of your moral window.

Your moral window. I once had a dream that contained seeds for a simple yet provocative idea about the *link* between moral sensations and a world beyond them. One night, I dreamed that a girl came up to me to ask a question: "What is the basis of a desire?" I had no idea where this question was coming from. So, I began to offer a complex and confusing answer. She just listened. Then I woke up.

As I reflected on my dream, a thought suddenly sprang into my mind: the basis of a desire is the sight of *something* good. The thought here is not that *everything* about every desire is good or that the desire itself is good. The thought, more precisely, is that when you desire something, your desire arises within you from a sense of something positive in its own right, like the positivity of a certain experience.[2]

This thought about desire provides a way to knit together two dimensions of the moral landscape. In the first dimension, we have moral *senses*, like the sense that it is good to feed the hungry. The second dimension goes beyond mere sense. It includes actual goodness. For example, it is *good* to feed the hungry. Your sense of goodness is your window into actual *goodness*, just as your sight of a chair is your window to an actual chair.

For the sake of neutrality, I express my proposal as a hypothesis:

The Moral Window Hypothesis: moral senses are senses *of* (windows into) moral aspects, like good, bad, positive, negative, right, and wrong.

To illustrate the hypothesis, let us consider some examples. Consider courage. Do you sense that courage is a virtue? If so, your sense of virtue is your window into a virtue.

Or take intellectual dishonesty: do you sense that intellectual dishonesty is *good*? Probably not. I predict you sense something negative about dishonesty. Perhaps you sense that dishonesty harms people, and perhaps you sense something problematic about harming people. Then, according to the Moral Window Hypothesis, your very sense of something problematic arises in you because you *see*—that is, sense—something actually problematic.

By your moral window, you can distinguish *some* good things from some bad things. Consider, for example, the following list: love, joy, peace, patience, kindness, and cruelty. If you are like me, you sense that one of the things on the list is not like the others. The Moral Window Hypothesis explains why: you sense that one of the items lacks a certain positive aspect that the others have.

[2]One version of this idea is developed in great detail by G. Oddie, *Value, Reality, and Desire* (New York: Oxford University Press, 2005).

Now to be clear, the Moral Window Hypothesis does not imply that people cannot make mistakes about what is good. You can see something faintly or imperfectly. For example, you may sense that cruelty is problematic but not see clearly the *root* of the problem. A lack of clear sight can lead to mistakes.

On this account, the moral window is like other "sense" windows. Each of your senses is a window into the world. Your visual sense, for example, is your window into a world with hills, trees, and rocks. Your hearing is your window into sounds produced by vibrations. Your sense of reason is your window into logical connections. Your sense of your own thoughts is a window into your inner mental life. And so on. In the same way, I propose for your consideration that when you sense moral qualities like good and bad, you are aware of some moral qualities.

Here, briefly, are two favorable consequences of the Moral Window Hypothesis. First, it makes sense of our moral language. We talk as if we already *think* some actions are actually wrong. For example, we say that rape, murder, and slavery are wrong, independently of whether people happen to want those things. None of those things are desirable *for their own sake*. None are good.

Consider, by contrast, how we talk about private preferences. You might prefer one flavor of ice cream, while I might prefer another. We do not debate which ice cream one *should* prefer—not seriously, anyway. Instead, we say that people may enjoy different desserts. When it comes to morality, on the other hand, people do seriously debate it. People talk as if some preferences, such as a preference for slavery, are *wrong*. The Moral Window Hypothesis makes sense of this way of talking.

If, on the other hand, morality is merely a matter of preference, it is unclear why anyone should work to help others. To solve any "problem," all one needs to do is stop feeling it is a problem. In fact, we could solve *all* the world's problems just by agreeing that no problems exist and removing our sense of distaste for current problems (like disease, cruelty, or kidnapping). Yet we don't ordinarily think about moral problems this way.

Instead, ordinary thinking includes the thought that problems extend beyond one's own personal feelings. When Bob thinks slavery should be stopped, for example, he is not merely thinking about *himself*, that is, that *he* dislikes or disapproves of slavery. Bob is thinking that slavery itself is a problem, even when he is not around to think about it.[3]

TESTING THE MORAL WINDOW

Of course, ordinary thinking is not always correct thinking. You may have doubts about whether the Moral Window Hypothesis is true. That's okay—*objectively*! Here I wish to emphasize that even if the moral landscape is entirely reducible to subjective experiences, still, the existence of moral experiences themselves are a significant dimension of the moral landscape. This single dimension is enough to inspire our inquiry into the foundation of moral experience (as we shall see).

In this section, I would like to consider some common objections to the Moral Window Hypothesis. These objections present barriers to "seeing" through one's moral window. My hope is to remove barriers that may block your moral window.

Objection 1. People have different moral opinions. If moral sense is a window to a moral landscape, then why do people "see" different things?

Response. The moral landscape has many crevices. To illustrate, when my three-year-old daughter, Chloe, would pull her sibling's hair, Chloe would laugh hysterically. No doubt her feeling of hysteria had *some* positive aspects. Laughing feels good. Yet Chloe failed to understand her sibling's perspective. Thus, if Chloe thought pulling her sibling's hair was good, we can understand why: it was because Chloe was more aware of the good aspects (e.g., her own happiness) than the negative aspects (her sibling's pain).

Take a more grown-up example. When we battle over politics, we are sorting through many, many moral aspects—and not everyone sees the same moral aspects with the same clarity. Each person has their own life story, which provides a unique lens through which to interpret political concepts and principles. Hence, disagreement happens.

Consider, moreover, that some aspects of the moral landscape are just harder to see. While it may be easy for us to sense a positive aspect of our *own* experience of pleasure, for example, it takes more work to

[3]For a clear-minded defense of ordinary thinking with respect to moral propositions, see M. Huemer, *Ethical Intuitionism* (New York: Palgrave, 2005).

understand complex aspects outside our own heads. For example, what are the moral connections between state authority and violations of non-aggression? Answering this question is like digging under the sea. Most people don't go under the sea.

The positivity of pleasure and the negativity of pain, by contrast, are far easier to see. Seeing these things is like looking up at the blue sky. People across time and culture easily see that pleasure has a certain positivity that pain lacks.

The Moral Window Hypothesis accounts for all these observations. After all, we can see *some* aspects of a moral landscape without seeing all of them with equal clarity. We don't need to see everything perfectly to see some things imperfectly.

Objection 2. Senses can create the illusion of sight. For example, in a dream, you can sense a landscape of shapes and colors. Obviously, the dream is only an illusion: the shapes and colors you sense are not there. Similarly, maybe moral sensations create an illusion. You sense good and bad, yet the good and bad are not there. How can anyone be sure moral senses are not illusory?

Response. My response, in short, is that *some* moral experiences cannot be an illusion because they involve direct awareness of good things *within you*. For example, when you experience a state of peace, you can sense something positive about that peaceful feeling within you. You sense this positive aspect directly. No inference is required.

The reason no inference is required is that you are directly aware of your own experiences. Even if you are hallucinating, you can detect aspects of your hallucination. For example, you can distinguish a hallucination of a pink rat from a hallucination of a blue bear. While no pink rat exists, still, the pink-rat sensation exists within you. The sensation *itself* has aspects. By sensing your own senses, you sense aspects of them, including positive and negative aspects.

Consider, for example, a feeling of peace. You can focus on your peaceful feeling and sense some of its aspects. You can sense, for example, that peace has a positive aspect.

To be clear, two disclaimers are in order. First, I'm not saying that *every* aspect of a positive experience is positive. A pleasure, for example, may have many aspects, some positive and others negative.

Second, I am not saying that you can *directly* detect every part of the moral landscape. I think some parts of the moral landscape require inferences that go beyond immediate experience. I want to be very clear: while some aspects require inferences, it does not follow that you cannot directly detect *any* aspects of the moral world.

On the contrary, you can directly detect some positive aspects of your own sensations. You can directly detect, for example, your own peaceful feelings, and you can compare peaceful feelings with painful feelings to see a difference in their positive aspects. If *anything* in the world is clear, it is that you can sense some good things within you.

One more clarification: the *aspects* of your senses differ from your *sense* of those aspects. You may sense, for example, that seeking falsehood is dangerous. Yet your sense of danger is not *itself* dangerous. In fact, the sense of danger is the opposite of dangerous; it protects you. In general, your sense *of* an aspect (of danger, positivity, goodness) is not the same as a sense that *has* that aspect (e.g., a dangerous sense).

I am drawing attention to the moral order *within your own senses* because you have the clearest vision of the moral order within you. Awareness of the positivity of peace, for example, is like awareness of a feeling of hunger. In both cases, your awareness is direct. Even if you are in a vivid dream, you can be aware of a hungry feeling or a positive emotion. You can see these things within you clearly.

Objection 3. Moral sensations come from evolution, not sight of actual moral qualities. Beings without the sense of danger, for example, die out. Hence, beings with moral sensations are more likely to survive. No deeper explanation is required.

Response. I will begin by acknowledging something right about the objection. I think it is right that an evolutionary history can explain, on some level, the development of moral sensations (putting the Hard Problem of consciousness aside).

Still, it would be a mistake to infer that your senses are therefore completely illusory. Consider that *all* your senses have a history. A visual sense of a lion, for example, may help a creature survive in the face of danger. It does not follow, however, that no lions exist.

As far as reason reveals, your visual sense could have an evolutionary history *and* be a window into the actual world. The same is so for every sense, including your sense of good and bad.

Consider, moreover, that the risk of illusion goes away when you are *directly aware* of something. For example, if you have a happy experience, you can be directly aware of the happiness within you. That's how you can be sure you have a happy feeling: you witness the feeling directly.

More to the point, you can directly detect positive aspects within you. You can detect, for example, that happiness has a positive aspect to it. Evolution does nothing to prevent this detection. Evolution prepares for it.

The way to build knowledge is to start with what is clear. What is clear to you? Is it clear that rational thinking has no more virtue than irrational thinking? Is it clear that kindness is no better than cruelty? Is it clear that happiness, peace, and love are as negative as depression?

I will tell you what is clear *to me*. It is clear that I sense at least some positive and negative emotions within my own experiences. As surely as true differs from false, it is clear to me that good differs from bad. It is clear that rational thinking and irrational thinking are not equally virtuous. It is clear that intellectual dishonesty does not deserve a badge of honor.

What is *not* clear to me, by contrast, is any good reason to doubt my moral senses. I have never seen any "good" reason to think that all moral aspects—positive and negative, good and bad, right and wrong—are completely absent from everything.

The safest path to truth extends from what is clear: some emotions, thoughts, and actions are clearly positive, good, or right, while others are clearly not.

Objection 4. Elementary schools around the world teach us the facts about opinions. One of the facts we all learn is that statements about good and bad are mere opinions. Hence, no moral facts exist.

Response. I have good news: we are free to question what people teach us. Test truth for yourself. Question everything. See more.

Ironically, the elementary school statements are themselves *assumptions*—mere opinions. While many teachers repeat these statements authoritatively as if they are facts, their "facts" about opinions are not themselves facts.

Consider what a fact is. A fact is about actual reality, independently of what people may believe. Opinions, by contrast, are only *beliefs*, which can vary from person to person. For example, some people believe the moral landscape is not real, while I believe it is.

Facts transcend your beliefs. Your *belief* that two plus two equals four, for example, arises from a sense—a window—within you. Yet the equation you sense transcends your belief: two plus two has the feature of equaling four with or without *your belief*. Similarly, you may have a sense of seeing a world with your eyes. The sense of sight is another window within you, whereas the world transcends your visual window. In the same way, the sense of right and wrong is in you, while the rightness and wrongness of things transcends your moral window.

You may have heard it said that it is a *fact* that the earth is round, while it is a mere *opinion* that certain things are good or bad. Yet I tell you that eating babies for fun is wrong—*really wrong*. Eating babies is as wrong as the earth is round.

Don't take *my* word for it.

Objection 5. Here is one more objection, which may be a root of many of the others. In the early twentieth century, some philosophers proposed that moral statements don't count as "factual" because they are not testable by the five senses.[4]

To illustrate, consider the statement that *ants have six legs*. This statement counts as factual. Factual statements, they proposed, are verifiable by the five human sense organs—eyes, ears, nose, tongue, and skin. It is factual, then, that ants have six legs because you can *see* ants with six legs. By contrast, statements, such as *cruelty is bad*, are not factual. You cannot test them by any of the five senses. Even statements about your own thoughts come under suspicion, since you sense your thoughts through an *inner* sense, not by the external organs listed. This theory of "factual"—sometimes called "verificationism"—filled academic halls with moral skepticism.

The objection, then, is this: factual statements are all verifiable by the five sense organs. Moral statements are not verifiable by the five sense organs. Therefore, moral statements are not factual.

---

[4]For history and variations of this thought, see T. Uebel, "Vienna Circle," *Stanford Encyclopedia of Philosophy* (2014), https://plato.stanford.edu/entries/vienna-circle/.

Response. Verificationism turns out to have a fatal vice: it is *false*. Consider first that verificationism is not *itself* verifiable through your eyeballs, ears, nose, tongue, or skin. You cannot see with your mere eyes that factual statements *cannot* be moral. Sniffing obviously won't help you verify verificationism. Nor does licking, touching, or bending your ear. In other words, verificationism fails to meet its own requirement for being factual. Hence, verificationism cannot be factual.

Moreover, verificationism contradicts other things we know. If verificationism is true, then the foundations of science—which include logic, probability theory, and growing branches of mathematics—all fail to be factual. Yet we understand the principles of math and logic by our sense of reason, not by mere eyes, ears, nose, mouth, or skin. So verificationism fails.

Fortunately, philosophers got wiser. We abandoned the strictest forms of verificationism. We moved on.[5]

Yet vapors of verificationism still permeate many sectors of society. In these sectors, moral skepticism fills the atmosphere. This atmosphere clouds minds. It blocks people from seeing even the *possibility* of a real moral landscape.

In this brief introduction, I hope I have helped clear away some obstacles to a moral landscape. At the very least, I hope you will be inspired to appreciate the positive aspects within your own experiences.

I will close this introduction to the moral landscape by noting an irony in denying the existence of a moral landscape. The irony is about the *motivation* to deny anything. To deny anything requires some motivation, some desire. Yet what is the basis of a desire?

To echo an idea from a dream, the basis of a desire is the sense of something good. When you desire to eat, for example, you sense something *good* about eating. Even if the food you desire is not healthy for you, still, the desire aims at *something* appealing—a *good* taste experience perhaps.

In the same way, a desire to deny the reality of all goodness aims at something good, like the goodness of saying something you think is

[5]Uebel, "Vienna Circle." According to a survey in 2009, a majority of philosophers surveyed favor some form of *moral realism*—i.e., the reality of moral qualities in the actual world (PhilPapers Surveys, https://philpapers.org/surveys).

true. If that is true, then you cannot desire to deny all goodness unless you sense some goodness in your very aim.

To conclude this section, I will pose a backup idea for the sake of modesty. My backup idea is that you can desire some things *for their own sake*. For example, suppose you desire to have vanilla ice cream. On one level, the basis of that desire is that you prefer vanilla. But that preference is not the *full* basis. On a deeper level, the basis of your preference is the *positivity* of a certain taste. A positive taste is itself desirable *for its own sake*. While different things taste differently to different people, the *positivity* of a taste is desirable for all people—or so I propose.

In this sense, we could use the term *good* to label aspects that are desirable for their own sake. My modest proposal, then, is that some aspects of reality are good in this minimal sense (at least).

MORAL FOUNDATION

Like a material landscape with various hills, trees, and rocks, a "moral" landscape has various moral textures. Moral textures include moral experiences, like the experience of good and bad, right and wrong, better and worse, positive and negative. These textures characterize some of your experiences. When you have a sense that something is wrong, for example, the sense itself is real. Moral experiences, then, comprise one dimension of the moral landscape. The other dimension of the moral landscape includes the moral qualities you sense through your moral window. So the moral landscape has two dimensions: (1) moral senses and (2) moral qualities.

The existence of a moral landscape (of either dimension) inspires a question: why is there a moral landscape? Why is anything good? Why is there even the *sensation* of good? Can the particles that comprise a material landscape, with dirt and trees, produce standards of good and bad, right and wrong? How?

On one level, we might think the answer is trivial: morality is basic and unexplained. Kindness, for example, is good, but nothing *makes* kindness good. Kindness is just good, and that's it. No deeper explanation is necessary. So where is the puzzle?

The deeper puzzle, however, is about how any moral framework could exist at all. Why, or how, does our reality contain *anything* good or bad? And why does the world contain any beings like us, who have any concept of good or bad, right or wrong?

We can easily imagine a world with mindless particles or with amoral machines. That is not our world, though. Our world contains beings whose lives deserve protection. Our world contains principles of justice. How? How is there any moral landscape anywhere, ever?

These questions take us back to the foundation of all things. I propose for your consideration that the foundation of the world is the foundation of both dimensions of the moral landscape. According to this theory, the foundation of existence has a moral nature that provides the basic materials for the moral landscape. In short, the moral landscape has a moral foundation.

To investigate this proposal, we can use a prediction test. In science, one way to test competing hypotheses is to consider how well those hypotheses predict observations. For example, climate change models that more clearly predict actual observations are more likely to be true. The more accurate the predictions, the more probable the hypothesis. We can apply this test to the moral foundation hypothesis.

To begin the test, consider what a moral foundation predicts. A moral foundation predicts certain things that flow from its moral nature. In particular, the moral nature includes basic moral qualities, like goodness, value, and the power to distinguish right from wrong.

Building upon previous steps from previous chapters, we can see that a moral foundation also has the resources of a foundational *mind*. As such, it has the power to *aim* for a certain sort of world. Just as an artist can paint a picture, a moral mind can paint a morally textured universe with other moral beings. A morally textured universe is just the sort of thing we may expect a moral foundation to create.

Without a moral foundation, by contrast, we have a prediction problem. Non-moral materials do not predict any moral texture. Suppose the foundation is nothing but molecules in motion. Then all you ever have is molecules in motion. Molecules collide to form new patterns. How do moral qualities, like good or bad, arise from purely non-moral components?

Even if we could conceivably build a moral quality out of amoral particles, still, what do particles *predict*? Do particles *predict* moral sensations? I do not see how. Without moral materials, nothing has any value, any sense of value, or any power to aim at anything valuable. Therefore, without moral materials, the foundation is composed of purely amoral materials, and there is literally no reason to expect—or predict—the existence of anything but amoral effects.

A foundation with a moral nature, by contrast, anchors the moral landscape. A moral foundation *predicts* both dimensions of a moral landscape. First, a moral foundation predicts the existence of moral beings who can sense moral qualities. Second, a moral foundation predicts the existence of moral qualities themselves, since its nature includes the basic moral qualities. From these basic qualities within the nature of the foundation, the foundation has the resources to create a moral world.

I have four stakes to hammer down this "moral foundation" step:

First stake: a moral foundation can make sense of *abstract moral principles*.

To illustrate an abstract moral principle, consider the principle that justice is a virtue. The virtuousness of justice does not depend on you, or me, or any particular pattern of particles. Rather, justice is a virtue whether or not any particles exist. According to *moral Platonists*, justice is an eternal, abstract form. It exists as an eternal, abstract reality.[6]

My purpose is not to battle moral Platonism. I wish only to point out how a moral foundation can anchor an abstract moral reality, assuming there is an abstract moral reality. Here is how: the foundation's moral nature *is* the abstract moral reality. The foundation includes within its nature principles of justice, principles of virtue, and principles of well-being. These principles constitute a moral standard rooted in the nature of the foundation of all things. In short, the abstract good is the nature of a moral foundation.

By anchoring abstract principles to the nature of a foundation, we have resources to explain—and predict—the *entire* moral order. First, we can explain the moral principles within the moral order: those principles flow from the most basic aspects included within the nature of a moral foundation.

Moreover, a moral foundation explains how moral agents, like us, can understand moral principles. A moral foundation can produce a world

[6]See P. E. More, *Platonism* (London: Princeton University Press, 1917), 217.

with moral communities. This power within the fabric of the foundation empowers the foundation to aim to create a world with a diversity of valuable beings. A foundation with a moral nature, then, predicts both abstract moral principles *and* the power to create a world with beings who can discover those principles.

The moral foundation has an advantage over the theory that there are abstract moral principles with *no foundation*. The moral foundation explains more. It explains why there are beings like us who can know about moral principles. The moral foundation has the resources to make a world with beings like us. The moral principles within the moral foundation are *reasons* to make a world like us, and the foundation has the power to act on those reasons. Without a moral foundation, by contrast, nothing predicts beings like us. Moral Platonism by itself predicts nothing like us.

Second stake: the moral foundation theory is a foundation for *all* the major moral theories, including consequentialism, contractarianism, constructivism, deontology, virtue ethics, universally preferable behavior, and other "secular" theories of morality.[7] These theories each provide a particular compass for navigating the moral landscape. Take whichever compass you wish.

My goal here is not to dispute the reliability of any particular moral compass. Rather, I aim to highlight a foundation that lays underneath all these theories of the moral landscape.

A moral foundation provides the basic materials for any moral theory. On all the theories listed, the world has moral textures: that is to say, some things are right, good, and healthy. A moral foundation explains how *any* moral textures could ever exist anywhere, ever. Like the soil inside a mountain, the foundation's moral nature is the soil for a moral landscape, no matter its precise shape.

Third stake: people can know that something is good without knowing the ultimate *source* of goodness.

To illustrate, when you walk up a mountain, you do not see all the soil inside the mountain. You can step up the mountain without any clue what is holding you up. In the same way, you can walk across the moral landscape without knowing about its foundation. For example, you can

---

[7]For a survey of moral theories, see M. Timmons, *Moral Theory: An Introduction* (Lanham, MD: Rowman & Littlefield, 2013).

know that kindness is good without having any thought about the ultimate foundation of goodness. In general, one can see a moral landscape without seeing its foundation.

I make this point to ensure we stand clear of a certain objection to the existence of a moral foundation. I have heard people object to a moral foundation by saying that people can be good without knowing anything about a foundation of goodness. My response is to clarify that yes, we can be good without knowing about the foundation of goodness. It would be a mistake, though, to infer that goodness has no foundation.

I offer one more, related clarification. Some people have said that certain things are good only *because* of their relation to the foundation. I am *not* saying that. When I say that goodness exists in the foundation's nature, I do not mean to imply that something is good *in virtue of* existing in the foundation's nature. Instead, I think goodness is a *basic* element of the foundation.

The principles of goodness are like pillars in a castle. The pillars don't exist *in virtue of* being in the castle. Rather, they are basic pieces of the castle; they help make the castle what it is. In the same way, principles of goodness help make the foundation what it is.

Final stake: good and bad are *asymmetric*. Bad depends on good. In order to experience something bad, there must already be something good to destroy or harm. For example, harming a person is bad precisely because a person has value, which is good. Good, by contrast, does not necessarily depend on bad. For example, someone could experience the good qualities of well-being and peace. These particular good qualities do not require any bad qualities. Good stands prior to all bad.

Consider, moreover, that the basic moral principles—of justice, virtue, well-being, and so on—are themselves good, not bad. To be clear, the principle provides a standard that *distinguishes* between good and bad, but this standard is itself good. A moral foundation, then, would include something good within its nature. By including something good, the moral foundation does not thereby include anything bad.

SUMMARY

The foundation of the world is the foundation of all moral textures—good, bad, right, wrong, negative, and positive. These moral textures comprise a moral landscape with two dimensions: (1) the sense of moral qualities and (2) the moral qualities themselves. A moral foundation makes sense of the existence of both dimensions. A moral foundation has moral materials that allow it to paint a morally textured world. Moreover, a moral foundation also has the power to create a world in which other moral beings, like us, can discover the moral landscape.

CHAPTER 10

FOUNDATION OF REASON

The next step is about the foundation of *all reasoning*. To install this step, I will begin by probing the nature of mathematics (a paradigm place of reason). Then, I will show how the foundation of everything could provide a foundation for the nature of mathematics. Finally, I will use reason to reveal something special about reason itself.

MATHEMATICAL LANDSCAPE

Just as moral principles comprise a moral landscape, mathematical principles comprise a *mathematical landscape*. To see this landscape, look inside your own mind. Within your mind, you can see mathematical *principles*. For example, you can see the principle that *two plus two equals four*.

What are mathematical principles? What is their nature?

To help us with our inquiry, I want to draw attention to two features of the mathematical landscape. These features point to the *robust nature* of mathematics, which in turn will point us to the foundation of its robustness.

The first feature is about the *size* of the mathematical landscape: mathematics does not "fit" entirely in your own mind. The mathematical landscape includes infinitely many truths, and you don't see all of them. Before you were born, two plus two equaled four, triangles formed three angles, and four was even. While you witness these principles *within* your mind, the principles you see don't depend on your sight of them. The principles of math don't wait for you to see them.

Your mind is not unique in this respect. Mathematical principles were also true before *my* mind existed. Before I existed, the universe still had order, including the order of logic and mathematics. Before I existed, square circles *couldn't* pop into existence. Square circles were always impossible, even before any humans had any concept of a square or a circle. We invented symbols so that we could *communicate* mathematical principles, but the principles don't need to be communicated to be true. The mathematical landscape is like earth's landscape: it exists beyond our own heads.

Another way to see the transcendence of mathematics is to see the difference between your mathematical thoughts and *correct* mathematical principles. When you take a math exam, you can have many mathematical thoughts in your mind. You could *think*, for example, that some numbers add up to 1,231,231. But notice that a mathematical thought is not the same as a *correct* thought. Correct thoughts are more than mere thoughts. A thought is correct if it matches actual reality. A mathematical thought is correct, then, if it matches a mathematical reality. So, while you can see mathematical reality from within your mind, the principles of mathematics do not depend on your particular thoughts; math transcends you.

Here is a second, related feature of the mathematical landscape: the principles of mathematics are *constant*. Mathematical principles do not change from day to day. Yesterday, two plus two equaled four. Today, two plus two equals four. Tomorrow, two plus two will still equal four. The day and time are irrelevant: two plus two always equals four. All mathematical truths are like that: these principles are constantly true, even while we sleep. For this reason, if you take a math exam on Tuesday, the answers will be the same as they were on Monday. Math is constant.

Here, then, are two features of a mathematical landscape:

Feature 1 (size): The mathematical landscape extends beyond your mind.

Feature 2 (stability): The mathematical landscape is constant.

Together these features point to the robustness of mathematics. The principles of mathematics are more robust than a leaf, a pack of cells, or a human thought. Unlike breakable, temporary things, the mathematical landscape is unbreakable. Math cannot be created or destroyed.

Why does math have such robustness? This question points us to the *foundation* of mathematics.

MATHEMATICAL FOUNDATION

So, what could possibly explain the existence of a mathematical landscape? Can the foundation of all existence provide a foundation for the existence of a mathematical landscape? If so, how?

We are ready to see how. We have already seen that the foundation of all existence is a foundation for the mental and moral dimensions of existence. My proposal has been that mental and moral realities point to a mental and moral foundation. Interestingly, this very same foundation has precisely the right resources to explain the mathematical realm.

Allow me to explain. Consider first that the ultimate foundation has the right *nature*. The foundation's nature is perfectly robust. In the previous chapter, we saw that a foundation with a moral nature could include moral principles. Here I want you to see that, in the same way, a foundation with a *mathematical* nature could include mathematical principles. By anchoring the mathematical principles in the nature of the foundation, we explain the robustness of mathematical reality. The foundation of everything has constant, eternal existence (see chapter three). Therefore, its nature has constant, eternal existence. It follows that mathematical principles *within its nature* are constant. This result is right.

On this account, your sight of mathematical truths takes your mind into the nature of the foundation. Although you witness this mathematical nature from inside your mind, your mathematical senses are a window into a nature that extends beyond your mind.

There is more. A mathematical foundation also explains why mathematical principles are *thought-like*. Although math was always my favorite subject growing up, I never noticed its thought-like nature, not until well after I finished my PhD in philosophy. Then the obvious became obvious: *mathematical principles have the same structure as a thought*. For example, the principle that *two plus two equals four* has the same structure as the thought that *two plus two equals four*. Both the principle and the thought have the following two distinguishing features: (1) they are about something (e.g., numbers), and (2) they are the sort of thing that can be true or false. Every thought and every mathematical principle alike has these same features.

Why do they have the same structure?

Consider, by contrast, trees. Trees don't have the structure of a thought. Trees are not about anything. Trees cannot be true or false, either. The size of the tree makes no difference. A tree will not transform into a thought by growing more leaves or by reaching some great height. All trees of all sizes and shapes are incapable of being *true*. And, all trees of all sizes and shapes are incapable of being *about* anything.

In general, all shapes and sizes are equally insufficient materials for constructing a thought-like nature. Take *any* particles and arrange them in *any* shape, whether the shape of a tractor or a neuron. Their shape is not itself *about* anything. No shape is a thought-like nature.

So, why do mathematical principles have the same structure as a thought? Here is the *simplest* explanation: thoughts and principles have the same structure because *they have the same nature*.

Suppose we say instead that thoughts and principles comprise completely different categories. Then we multiply categories beyond necessity. The simpler—and more probable—theory is that thoughts and principles have the same structure because they have the same nature.

To be extra modest and careful, I will leave open whether principles *are* thoughts. My observation here is this: principles and thoughts are deeply similar. They have the same structure. By this observation, reason leads me to think at least this much: mathematical principles are thought-*like*—that is, they have the characteristic features of thoughts just mentioned.

How can *any* thought-like natures exist? A mental foundation accounts for how. A mental foundation has *foundational* thought-like elements. The mathematical landscape is thought-like, then, because it is rooted in a mind-like foundation. In this way, the mathematical landscape can have its foundation in the nature of a mathematical mind.

Consider, again, that thoughts and principles have the same structure. The thought that two plus two equals four has the same structure as the principle that two plus two equals four. A mathematical, mind-like foundation, then, explains the thought-like nature of math. A mental foundation has thought-like elements within its nature. Some of these thought-like elements are thought-like mathematical principles.

I have now installed the basic structure of this step to a mathematical foundation. Many books cover many theories of the foundations of mathematics,[1] and it is beyond my reach to canvas all those theories here. My goal is just this: I wish to display the resourcefulness of a mental foundation. A mental foundation provides construction materials for consciousness, matter, moral sensations, and moral qualities. In addition, a mental foundation provides the deepest possible explanation of the mathematical landscape.

Going Deeper

Here is an additional, advanced reason to think that mathematical principles flow from a mental foundation. It starts with a paradox discovered by Bertrand Russell.[2] This paradox is about propositions. It goes like this. Consider the following proposition, P: All the propositions that describe other propositions are about other propositions. Proposition P is very scary. Its very existence invites a contradiction into our universe. Here is why. P exists—I just stated it. Yet by logic, either P describes itself or not. Both options lead to a contradiction, as we shall see. Suppose, first, P describes itself. Then P is among the propositions it describes. Yet P only describes propositions about *other* propositions. Hence, P does not describe itself. But if P does not describe itself, then that means that P is *among* the propositions it describes (because P, by definition, describes all the propositions that do not describe themselves). Hence, P is a proposition that does describe itself if it does not. Either way, then, we have a contradiction—and the universe explodes (because *everything* follows from a contradiction).[3]

How do we avoid the contradiction?

---

[1]For an introduction to the philosophy of mathematics, see M. Colyvan, *An Introduction to the Philosophy of Math* (Cambridge: Cambridge University Press, 2012).

[2]B. Russell, *Principles of Mathematics* (Cambridge: Cambridge University Press, 1903).

[3]*Proof.* Suppose A and not A. Therefore, A. Therefore, A or Q (for any Q). Not A (by our supposition). Therefore, Q.

Over the years, I have found only one good solution to this paradox. The solution is this: at least some propositions have a *dependent nature*. Let me unpack why dependence is relevant. The standard theory of *independent* propositions is that propositions are eternal, independent, abstract objects. On this account, all propositions are eternally and automatically actual. We are now a single step away from the paradox. The only thing to add is that the paradoxical proposition, P, is paradoxical for one reason: P is eternal and automatically actual. Hence, P ends up describing itself, since it already exists among the propositions it describes. Yet P cannot describe itself. Hence, we fall into the contradiction.

We can avoid the contradiction by supposing—recognizing!—that at least some propositions have a dependent nature. Here is how this solution works. Dependent propositions don't automatically exist. More specifically, P doesn't automatically exist among the propositions it describes because P is dependent. For this reason, P does not describe itself. It can't. P only describes already-existing propositions—propositions that exist just prior to P. Hence, P does not describe itself, and no contradiction follows. We are paradox free.

This solution has dramatic ramifications concerning the ultimate source of propositions. Consider how a proposition could be dependent. What could a proposition depend on? Could a proposition depend on trees, atoms, or other arbitrary configurations of matter?

I am aware of only one "material" that could ever make a proposition: *concepts*. When you bring to mind the proposition that one plus two equals three, for example, you organize some concepts of some numbers together with the concepts of addition and equals. By organizing these concepts in a certain way, you grasp—or form—the proposition that one plus two equals three in your mind. I see no other way to form a proposition. I infer, then, that dependent propositions depend on prior concepts.

If instead we say that propositions can exist independently of prior concepts, then nothing stops propositions from "already" existing prior to all concepts. More to the point, nothing stops P from already existing among the propositions it describes—and the contradiction is back.

We might try to block the contradiction by letting P "wait" before coming to exist. For example, perhaps P comes into existence immediately after the propositions it describes already exist. But this idea compounds the mystery: how does P "know" to come into existence? Propositions don't themselves have the power to produce new propositions. Propositions entail existing propositions; they don't produce new ones. Therefore, if P exists after other propositions, something other than propositions is required to explain how.

A mental foundation has the resources to explain sequentially existing propositions. A mental foundation can conceptualize propositions just as we can. The simplest, most basic propositions can exist in a basic way within the nature of the foundation. The foundation can then make dependent propositions exist in a certain order by conceiving of propositions in a certain order, such as from basic to complex.

Here, then, is the argument. Propositions depend on prior concepts (to solve the paradox of propositions). Mathematical propositions exist prior to the concepts in creaturely minds (by the features of a mathematical landscape). Therefore, mathematical propositions depend on a foundational mind with foundational concepts.

THE NATURE OF REASON

Like mathematical principles, we recognize *principles of reason* in our own minds. For example, by reason we see that nothing is both true and false at the same time.

Why, however, do any principles of reason ever exist? Consider what principles of reason are. Principles of reason are principles that specify how *people* think correctly. *People*! Why does reality "care" to include any principles in the service of people?

Going Deeper

What are the principles of reason? Reason includes these classical laws:

1. The law of non-contradiction: for all A, A is not both true and not true.
2. The law of excluded middle: for all A, everything is either A, or not A.
3. The law of identity: for all A, A is A.

These laws are not the only principles of reason, though. Principles of reason govern correct thinking about many, if not all, natures, including the nature of numbers, sets, shapes, possibility, necessity, parts, wholes, dependence, minds, and reason itself. As far as reason reveals, reason's light has no limit.

Reason itself reveals the source of its light. Let us follow reason to its source. By reason, we have seen how an ultimate source of *all* dependent things could have the resources to produce a universe with minds, matter, morals, and mathematics. We are now ready to see how reason itself could exist.

Here is how. First, the foundation's resources include mental resources (see chapters seven through nine). Second, the foundation lacks arbitrary limits (see chapter six). It follows, by reason, that the foundation has mental resources without arbitrary limits. The only mentally resourceful nature without arbitrary limits is a nature that includes perfect rules of reasoning. Anything less than perfect has a limit with respect to its power to reason. A mental foundation without limits, then, has the power to reason perfectly.

Something special follows about the source of reason. Consider *where* the principles of reason exist. I am not talking about their location in space. I am talking about their "location" within a nature. Consider this: to reason perfectly is to follow the perfect principles of reason. Since the power to reason perfectly exists at the foundation of everything else, the principles of reason have only one place they can exist: in the foundation's nature. In other words, the foundation of perfect reasoning must include, within its nature, the perfect principles of reason.

By anchoring reason to the nature of the foundation, we can also explain why any of *us* can follow reason. For then there is literally a "reason" within the fabric of reality to create other minds who can discover the principles of reason. It is not trivial that there are minds. As we saw in chapter seven, producing minds from non-minds results in a construction problem: how could non-sensing materials ever *sense* any rules of reason? We also have a probability problem: even if mindless materials could sense reason, why would that be remotely probable? We have a solution: the foundation has both the mental resources and some good reasons to produce other minds.

Let us look closer at the *reasons* a foundational mind might have for creating other minds. Consider this. The foundation of reason is also the foundation of morals. The foundation of morals includes a moral nature that includes moral principles. For example, the moral foundation includes the self-evident principle that moral beings with minds are valuable beings. It also includes the principle that the exploration and discovery of truth via reason has value. These principles are themselves *reasons* to produce a world with other minds who can explore and discover things. If the foundation has these principles of reason within its nature, then the foundation has *reasons* to produce a world with other minds.

The existence of the principles of reason themselves independently confirms this same result. The principles of reason, like the propositions of mathematics, are themselves *thought-like* entities. Principles of reason, like all thoughts, are about things. The only clear examples of things that are about things are concepts and thoughts (or maps, graphs, or other representations that have their aboutness ultimately because of concepts and thoughts). Moreover, principles of reason, like mathematical principles, are *robust* (constant and eternal).

Consider what follows. The principles of reason are thought-like and robust. It follows—by the light of reason itself—that the foundation of reason is robust and thought-like.

Imagine, by contrast, a bunch of material stuff springing into existence from nothing, with no mind behind it. If people come only from mindless particles, then *reasoning* comes from non-reason. Every thought then ultimately arises from thoughtlessness. Moreover, the ultimate basis of all your thoughts is literally nonsense. That can't be right. These particles have no reason to produce people. Furthermore, packs of particles lack the power to be "aware" of principles of reason.

Here is the root of the problem. Without an ultimate mind, the following three things are missing from the foundation:

1. A reason to produce people
2. The resources to produce people
3. Principles of reason themselves

Without these things, there is, then, *no reason* for there to be reason anywhere, ever.

Yet we can see, by reason itself, that reason is real. From here, we can see—by reason—that reason does not spring from non-reason. Only one option remains: reason exists at the foundation of everything.

This result is special. It implies that anyone who follows reason is doing something special: when you follow reason, you are following logical lines within the fabric of the foundation. In other words, when you reason well, you draw your mind into the nature of the foundation. To be near reason is to be near the foundation.

This result also has an extra-special consequence for those who have followed reason away from a certain religion. Perhaps reason has set you free from a previous, limited way of thinking. What is this "reason" that guides you? I propose to you that anyone who follows reason far enough and long enough can discover that *true reason* is a special light at the foundation of everything. You can discover the light that leads you. You can discover the light that frees you.

By the light of reason, we can see that reason must exist *at the foundation*. Without reason at the ground layer, nothing *could* make sense. Nothing could have any order. Reason is foundational for all organization in the world and in your mind. Reason is before all things that have been made. Nothing that has been made has been made without its perfect light. Without reason, there is nothing: no math, no logic, and no *reason* to produce other minds. Reason frees your mind from errors so that you may discover the real greatness of the foundation of everything.

SUMMARY

The foundation of everything is a foundation of the most abstract dimensions of reality—math, logic, and reason. A *mental* foundation has exactly the right resources to explain the abstract dimensions. A mental foundation has a mental nature. This nature includes the thought-like principles that comprise mathematics and all proper reasoning.

If, instead, the foundation consists merely of mindless materials, then it lacks the thought-like principles of mathematics and logic. Then the foundation's nature does not predict any principles of proper thinking. Mindless matter predicts nothing but mindless matter. Moreover, mindless matter literally has *no reason* within it. It is mindless, after all. Thus, it has no reason to produce the sort of beings who can comprehend principles of reason.

A mental foundation, by contrast, has good reason to value interesting things, like minds that can value reason. It makes sense, then, that there are minds that can value reason—*if* there is a mental foundation.

These results fill out the nature of the foundation. The foundation is a foundation of both concrete and abstract dimensions of reality. The light of reason reveals how: by anchoring reason in the nature of the foundation, we can explain how the foundation of all existence can be the foundation of minds, matter, morals, math, and reason itself.

CHAPTER 11

PERFECT FOUNDATION

We have come a long way. With reason in hand, we first followed a path to the *foundation* of all existence. We began to attempt to *see into* the foundation's nature. By a sequence of steps, we stepped across five features of the foundation: (1) self-sufficiency, (2) independence, (3) necessity, (4) ultimacy, and (5) eternality. Then came our most abstract step, where we looked into the foundation's "pure actuality" (simplicity and inner purity). After that, we took several more steps to see how the foundation could connect with four dimensions of reality: (1) mental, (2) material, (3) moral, and (4) mathematical. Each of those steps required travelling across a huge field of inquiry. If that were not enough of an accomplishment, we *then* sought to understand the foundation of all reason.

Now here we are, a step away from something very special. All the steps together have been leading up to this final step, which will take us to the treasure at the end of the bridge of reason. It is time to put the final structure of our bridge in place.

In what follows, I will install an archway with inner lights. This piece will shine on the final step. The lights together expose from different angles the foundation's *deepest* attribute.

FROM PURELY ACTUAL TO PURELY POSITIVE

We will now look into the depths of the foundation. I will use "pure actuality" as a lens. In chapter six, we saw that the foundation has a purely actual nature. In this chapter, we will have a closer look at the *root* of pure actuality. What explains the foundation's pure actuality? I will seek the deepest possible explanation.

My goal is to reveal a link between pure actuality and *perfection*. I will first say what I mean by "perfection." Then I will show how perfection explains pure actuality.

Seeing perfection. We can see perfection through two lenses. Through the first lens, we see what perfection *lacks*: perfection lacks defects. I define *defect* as anything that detracts from a thing's value. For example, a car with a broken engine has a defect. Its broken engine detracts from the car's value. A perfect thing has no defects at all.

The second lens lets us see what perfection *has*: perfection has value. In the next section ("How to See Value"), I will say more about standards of value. In particular, I will make a distinction between value that *flows from* preferences (such as the value of your favorite color) and value that *explains* (or *flows to*) preferences (such as the value of persons).

For now, it suffices to highlight that different things have different value. Standards of value depend on the category of the object. When I talk about a perfect car, for example, I am talking about perfection in relation to a car. A perfect diamond, by contrast, is different. Its standards of perfection are different. A defect in a diamond may not be a defect in a car.

For the purpose of our discussion, I want to direct our attention to things with the *highest value*. Consider, for contrast, a Toyota Camry. This car has some value. However, if you want to get a car with even higher value, you can expand your search beyond the make and model of a Toyota Camry. You can consider a wider selection of vehicles made by Ford, BMW, Porsche, Lexus, and so on. From the wider selection, you have more power to choose a car with the best qualities. The car with the most possible value encompasses more value than the most valuable Toyota Camry (unless Toyota Camry happens to be the most valuable category of car!).

In general, *more value* means qualities that are *more positive*. A perfect car, for example, includes more positive qualities than the perfect Toyota Camry. Furthermore, a perfect car has the best combination of positive qualities that *any* car could have.

The *highest* value has the most positive qualities. I will call the highest value "absolute perfection"—or "perfection" for short. A perfect thing, then, is the greatest—most valuable—kind of thing. A perfect thing has no defects of any kind. It is purely positive. In other words, perfection implies *supreme value*.

How to see value. What does it mean to have value?

To answer this question, we need to see a distinction between two types of value. First, value can reflect *preference*. For example, if Sam likes chocolate ice cream, then chocolate ice cream has a positive—valuable—taste to Sam. This value reflects Sam's preference.

Another type of value is value that reflects a *nature*, independent from preference. Some examples: honesty, kindness, generosity, rationality, you. These things have value. Their value does not depend on someone's preference. In fact, their relationship to preference seems to me to go the other way. Kindness, for example, is not valuable just because someone happens to prefer it. Rather, you can be motivated to prefer kindness precisely because you can see that kindness has value. Kindness has value by nature, not by preference.

One could reject this idea. One could deny that any qualities have value by nature. Instead, all value, one might say, is purely subjective. On this view, a person is not valuable by nature; rather, a person is only valuable if someone happens to *prefer* that person's existence. Here all value reflects preference, taste, desire, or other subjective states. No quality is valuable in itself.

In a previous chapter (chapter nine), however, I sought to show the reality of some aspects of a moral landscape. My method was to remove some common obstacles to seeing a moral landscape through your moral window. Those obstacles are relevant to seeing *value*, since value is a basic aspect of the moral landscape. I hope that my discussion there could help remove at least some barriers to seeing value.

Here I will say a little more about how I think you can see valuable qualities. What I offer next are three methods by which I think people can see that some value is real. My hope is that these methods will be tools that may serve you in your own inquiry.

Method 1: By direct awareness. The easiest things to see are in your own mind. For example, you can see that two plus two equals four within your mind. You can see that sadness differs from happiness. You can see that a thought about rabbits is *about rabbits*. And so on. In all these cases, you have direct awareness of certain elements within your own experience.

I propose for your consideration that you also have the power to see *value* in your mind. Here is a test. Check to see if you have any positive emotions, like peace or happiness, within you. If you sense any positivity of any emotion, that positivity is itself value. Positivity is an example of what I *mean* by "value."

To be clear, I am not proposing that *every* aspect of *every* positive feeling is valuable. After all, people can feel happy about cruelty. Happiness can have many different aspects, positive and negative. Even still, happiness has *some* positive aspect, regardless of its source.

Here is another test. Consider your own self. I predict that you can *sense* some value by focusing on yourself. When you focus on yourself, you can sense some of the value you have as a person. You won't need to first decide to *prefer* yourself for you to have a positive aspect. It goes the other way: the value you sense is a basis for preferring your continued existence.

It is easy to miss the value of something if we think all value must come entirely from preference. But let us be careful to separate our *sense* from the *value* we sense.

To draw out the distinction between sensing value and the value sensed, consider a case where everyone fails to sense someone's value. Imagine Sue has no home, no friends, and no money. Would Sue then have *no value*?

It might be tempting to say that Sue would have value only because *we* think she does. However, there is more going on here. Yes, we sense that people have value. But that's not all we sense. Here is what I sense from my own perspective: I have the sense that people would have value *without my sense* of it. I sense that people have value while I sleep. Compare: two plus two equals four while I sleep. In the same way, you have value while you sleep, even if no one is sensing your value.

It can be easy to miss the difference between one's *senses* and the *properties* that one senses. The sense that jam tastes good, for example, is subjective: not everyone has that taste. Yet, the goodness of a particular taste is objective: everyone with *that* taste can—by direct awareness—detect its goodness.

To illustrate further, consider the following two hypothetical situations:

1. You are in a just society.
2. You like jam.

These situations differ: justice is about value, while jam is about your sense. While you might *like* them both, the sense of what you *like* differs from the sense of *value*. You may sense, in fact, that people *should* like justice, whether or not anyone does. By contrast, if you are like me, you do not sense that people should like jam. Your sense of liking jam—if you have that sense—is a sense about you, not about the value of jam's nature.

Here is the crucial point: your sense of value is a window into value. When you experience happiness, for example, your sense of happiness is a window into positive aspects of happiness. Although your happiness is subjective, its *positivity* is objective. In other words, the positive aspects of your positive experiences have *actual value*—and you can see this value within you by direct awareness.

Method 2: By uniformity. Suppose we say that the sense of "value" never detects any real value. Then we fall into a pit of skepticism about all our senses. Why think *any* sense detects anything? Perhaps all senses—visual, auditory, and so on—are all illusions.

If we say that only *some* senses are windows into reality but not others, then we break the uniformity of our senses. Suppose, for example, you trust your hearing but not your vision. You think hearing reveals real pitches, while vision reveals nothing. That would be silly. It would be silly because it would be arbitrary and unmotivated, unless one has some good reason to trust auditory sense but not visual sense.

In the same way, it is arbitrary and unmotivated to distrust one sense but not others *for no reason*. Without a principled reason to distinguish between the senses, we have no good reason to trust some senses but not others.

You might wonder whether moral sense could be importantly different from the visual sense. You might think that when it comes to moral sense, there is good reason to think this sense is a closed window.

I will briefly consider a sample of the reasons I have heard, along with my responses.

First, I have heard it said that we cannot trust our sense of value because evolution produced the sense of value for our survival.

My response: a biological history produced *all* our senses (if it produced any). Therefore, all senses are in the same boat: all are untrustworthy or trustworthy. Uniformity remains unbroken.

Second, I have heard it said that we cannot *test* our moral sense: for example, we cannot test that justice is a virtue using a scientific experiment.

My response: how do you "test" any sense? Tests themselves depend on senses. Your visual sense, for example, is your instrument to test aspects of a material landscape. Similarly, your moral sense is your instrument to test aspects of a moral landscape. If instead senses *first* depend on tests, while tests depend on senses, then we fall into a contradictory circle. Bad move.

Third, I have heard it said that the existence of actual value is not necessary to explain your sense of value, while the existence of an external material world is necessary to explain your visual sense.[1]

My response: this proposal rests on a mistake. It assumes moral sight requires an inference to the best explanation. That's not true: you can see value without having to explain anything. For example, you can see that you have value. You can see some value within you in the same way you see math—*by direct awareness.*

If we instead distrust our inner senses, then we have fallen into the deepest pit of skepticism—and there is no hope of ever getting out. We could not even know that we have thoughts or feelings. I have good news: the power of direct awareness protects us from falling into this pit of skepticism.

In the end, I am not aware of any good reason to break the uniformity of the senses. All senses alike are windows. What makes a sense a *sense* is that it is a sense *of* something: it is a window into something.

Maybe the temptation to break the uniformity of senses arises from the observation (or theory) that some senses are more reliable than others. To be clear, then, I am not suggesting that any senses

[1]See G. Harman, "Ethics and Observation," in *Ethical Theory 1: The Question of Objectivity*, ed. J. Rachels (Oxford: Oxford University Press, 1998), 85-91.

are perfectly reliable. Senses can mislead us. Still, unless one has a reason to think that one's sense is misleading, the sense itself is evidence of the thing you sense. You don't need *perfect* sight to have *some* sight.

Instead of building our understanding on what is unclear, we can build our understanding on what is clear. So, what is clear? Speaking from my perspective, it is clear that some experiences have some positive aspects. It is clear, for example, that the experience of contentment has certain positive aspects that are missing from torture. It is clear that rational thinking is a better quality of thinking than dishonest or irrational thinking.

As with anything, we can entertain the possibility that all our senses are misguided. True. Still, unless we have some reason to think we *are* mistaken, our sense of value is itself a reason—a *valuable* reason—to think some value is real.

Method 3: By desire. As I noted in chapter nine, denying the reality of all value leads to an irony. If I deny the reality of value, then, to be consistent, I must deny that my *denial* has any value. Once I see that my denial of all value has no value, however, then what could motivate me to continue to deny all value? How could I *desire* to deny value once I see there is absolutely no value in doing so?

Clever people will find clever answers. But if we want the *truth*, we must consider whether the clever answers are true.

It seems to me that denying the existence of value is like denying the existence of meaning. Denying meaning is self-defeating: the statement that *no statements have meaning* is itself meaningless if it is true. So why think it? It seems to me that denying value is similarly self-defeating: the belief that *nothing has value* has no value if it is true. So why endorse that belief?

The problem in both cases is about motivation. The statements defeat one's motivation to endorse them. You wouldn't endorse that *no statements have meaning* unless some part of you thought that your endorsement had meaning. Similarly, you wouldn't endorse that nothing has value unless some part of you thought your endorsement had some value.

The *root* of the problem, it seems to me, is that desires have a basis. When you desire to seek truth, for example, your desire for truth has some basis. What is that basis? By inner reflection, it seems to me that the basis of every desire is the *sight of some value.*

To illustrate, ask yourself why you have any desire. I predict you will notice that all your desires are desires *for* something. For example, you may desire to eat. This desire is for a certain experience, such as the experience of satisfying your hunger or the experience of a sweet taste. Ultimately, the thing you have a desire for is something you perceive to have some positive aspect. For example, this experience of satisfying your hunger has a positive aspect. This positive aspect—that is, *value*—is the basis of your desire.

To be clear, I am not suggesting that the basis of a desire is always *entirely* positive. Far from it. My suggestion, rather, is that the reason you would desire anything is because you sense *something* positive, whether a taste, a pleasure, or a positive experience. Positive aspects may not *justify* every desire, but they are part of the basis of every desire. In this way, desires point to some value.

From value to perfection. We are now ready to consider the value of the foundation of everything. How much value does the foundation have? Any?

Let us first consider the hypothesis that the foundation has *no* value. Then the foundation has no positive aspects of any kind. On this theory, the foundation is either completely neutral or completely negative.

However, the foundation cannot be completely neutral or completely negative. If the foundation has no value, then we have a construction problem: how can value arise from completely value-less materials?

I'll offer two reasons why I think value cannot spring from complete non-value. First, the very power to produce value is itself valuable. Consider your power to serve people. Your very power to serve people is a valuable feature of you. It allows you to add value to the world. The ability to add value is valuable. The ultimate foundation has the ultimate ability to add value to the world, since it obviously had the ability to add *you* to the world. Therefore, the ultimate foundation must have at least some value.

Here is another reason I think the foundation has value. The foundation has value in virtue of its valuable attributes. For example, the foundation's nature includes the rules of reason (see chapter ten). Rules of reason are themselves valuable, since they protect us from harm. Also, the foundation's nature includes the moral standard (see chapter nine). A moral standard has value, and therefore, the foundation's nature has value.

Suppose, then, that the foundation has value. How much value might it have?

The previous steps prepare us for a clear answer. We can now build on the "pure actuality" step. By pure actuality, the foundation *lacks limits* (see chapter six). By reason, then, the foundation lacks limits in value. The foundation has *some* value (by the two reasons just given). Therefore, the foundation must have value without limit.

How can something have value without limit? My answer takes us to the deepest attribute of the foundation. The foundation has value without limit by *being perfect*.

This result follows from my definition of "perfect" as something that (1) lacks defects and (2) has supreme value.[2] The foundation has no defects, for a defect is a limit in some positive (valuable) respect, and the foundation has no limit in value. And the foundation has supreme value because anything less would mark a limit in its total value. In this sense, the foundation is *purely positive*—without any inner limit or imperfection. So, it is perfect.

HOW TO BE PERFECT

Absolute perfection is the most powerful property conceivable. From perfection flows the ultimate basis of *every* positive quality. In previous chapters, we've seen that the foundation has many positive qualities. Yet we have not considered all its positive qualities. It is now time to complete our picture of the perfect foundation by deducing some additional positive qualities.

Consider again what it means to be perfect. To be perfect is to be purely positive. A perfect foundation includes the greatest conceivable concentration of positive qualities.

[2]For a related analysis of the nature of perfection, see G. Oppy, *Describing Gods* (Cambridge: Cambridge University Press, 2014), 62-86. We can put my analysis of perfection in Oppy's terms: perfection is *idealized excellence*.

We could call a perfect foundation "maximally great." The term "maximally great" describes the highest degree of greatness. The relationship between maximal greatness and perfection is like the relationship between the highest mountain on earth and Mount Everest. Mount Everest *is* the highest mountain on earth. Similarly, absolute perfection *is* the highest degree of greatness. It is the highest value.

In order for something to be maximally great, it must have great-making features to the highest degree. I will deduce three classic examples: maximal power, maximal knowledge, and maximal goodness. I will show how these properties flow from a maximally great—*perfect*—foundation.[3]

Maximal power. How powerful is the foundation? The foundation has at least some power (see chapter four). The foundation has no arbitrary boundaries, gaps, or limits (see chapter six). Therefore, the foundation's power cannot be arbitrarily limited. It has unlimited, maximal power (or as much power as is consistent with the highest value).[4]

Does the foundation have the power to produce an *unliftable* stone? The answer depends on whether the existence of such a stone is *possible*. After all, the foundation is the foundation of all *possible* things, not *impossible* things. If an unliftable stone is possible, then it is possible for the foundation to create such a stone, but not possible for anything to lift it (by definition of "unliftable"). If, on the other hand, an unliftable stone is an impossible stone, then—by definition—no possible power can create it. The solution, then, is that the foundation has *possible* powers, not *impossible* powers.[5]

Notice that the lack of an impossible power is not an *arbitrary* limit. The foundation is perfect, without arbitrary limits. It is not an arbitrary

---

[3]On this account, maximal greatness flows from a more basic concept of supreme value (pure positivity). This account provides a *root* for the concept of the greatest possible being. See J. Speaks, *The Greatest Possible Being* (Oxford: Oxford University Press, 2018), 1-18.

[4]Cf. R. Koons, "A New Look at the Cosmological Argument," *American Philosophical Quarterly* 34 (1997): 193-212.

[5]Cf. T. Aquinas, *Summa theologiae*, trans. Fathers of the English Dominican Province (New York: Benzinger, 1948), I.25. See also A. J. Fredosso and T. Flint, "Maximal Power," *The Existence and Nature of God*, ed. A. J. Fredosso, 81-113 (Notre Dame: University of Notre Dame Press, 1983) for a more sophisticated analysis of "maximal power." But see G. Oppy, "Omnipotence," *Philosophy and Phenomenological Research* 71, no. 1 (2005): 58-84 for a critique, and K. Pearce and A. Pruss, "Understanding Omnipotence," *Religious Studies* 48, no. 3 (2012): 403-14 for further developments. Rather than attempt to analyze "maximal power" in terms of non-power (like "possible action"), here I propose to understand maximal power as simply the greatest possible power.

limit to be unable to do impossible things. Lacking impossible power doesn't detract from perfection. On the contrary, the lack of an impossible power flows from perfection.

Here is another way to see that perfection precludes impossible powers. Suppose the foundation had an impossible power. Then its nature would be *incoherent* (i.e., inconsistent with reason), since it would have a power that nothing can have. Incoherence is itself a defect. It defies reason. The foundation has no defects. Hence, the foundation cannot have incoherence. Hence, it cannot have impossible powers.

In summary, the foundation's power is *maximal.* Anything less than maximal is an arbitrary limit. The perfect foundation is not arbitrary. Instead, the perfect foundation is the *least arbitrary, least limited* way a foundation could be. Therefore, a perfect foundation has maximal possible power.

Maximal knowledge. I will now show three different ways to deduce maximal mentality.

Reason 1: From power. First, maximal knowledge is deducible from maximal power. Here is how. A perfect foundation has maximal possible power (see above). Among the possible powers is the power to know something. Therefore, a perfect foundation has the power to know something. Only minds have the power to know something. Therefore, the foundation has a mind.

Next, the foundation's mind cannot be *less than maximal.* Anything less than maximal would imply arbitrary limits. If, for example, the foundation's mind could only know mathematical truths but not moral truths, then its ability to know truths would be limited with respect to a positive quality. A perfect foundation has no limits with respect to any positive quality (by its pure actuality). Therefore, a perfect foundation has unlimited, maximal knowledge.[6]

Notice that this deduction sidesteps all my other arguments for a mental foundation. I gave arguments for a mental foundation from minds, matter, morals, and mathematics. We may put those arguments

---

[6]This pathway may remind you of an ontological argument for a maximal being. However, instead of proceeding purely a priori (as an ontological argument does), we proceed a posteriori (by existence) to deduce the foundation of actual existence. We then apply three different tools (simplicity, explanatory depth, and uniformity) to uncover pure actuality—from which we now deduce maximality via conceptual analysis.

aside here. The current deduction doesn't use any of them. Instead, the argument takes an independent path, going from perfect power to the powers of a perfect mind.

The independence of this path helps make this final step more secure. We don't *need* the previous steps. To help us be sure we are on solid ground, I will attempt to uncover two more supports next.

Reason 2: From value. A perfect foundation is purely positive—that is, maximally valuable. Knowledge is itself valuable. The more knowledge, the more value. Hence, a maximally valuable foundation has maximal knowledge. If its knowledge were arbitrarily limited, then it would not be *maximally* valuable. Hence, its knowledge is not arbitrarily limited. It is maximal.

I propose you can see this result by direct insight into the value of knowledge. Just as you can see that two plus two equals four by direct insight into these numbers, you can see that a maximally valuable foundation would have maximal knowledge by direct insight into the value of knowledge.

Reason 3: From reason. This final support builds on the previous chapter on the foundation of reason. Previously, I argued that reason itself is an aspect of a mind-like foundation. My argument, in summary, was that only a perfect mind could include the perfect rules of reasoning within its nature. Rules of reasoning are about perfect reasoning, after all. If that is correct, then to have a nature with the rules of reason is to have a nature with rules of perfect reasoning. It follows that the foundation of reason is a perfect mind.

Maximal goodness. The foundation is either bad, good, or morally neutral. The foundation cannot be *bad* because it is perfect. Recall (from chapter nine) that good and bad are asymmetric: the foundation of a moral landscape is itself good, not bad. Moreover, a perfect foundation is purely positive, while a bad foundation is not purely positive. Badness is negative. Therefore, a perfect foundation lacks badness.

Similarly, a perfect foundation cannot be merely neutral. A perfect foundation is *purely positive.* Pure positivity precludes complete neutrality. Therefore, the perfect foundation is neither bad nor neutral. Instead, the perfect foundation is perfectly good.

THE UNIFYING POWER OF PERFECTION

Perfection unifies all the attributes of the foundation. Perfection is the deepest attribute from which all positive attributes flow. From this singular aspect arises the foundation's moral nature (to act perfectly), its mathematical nature (to reason perfectly), and its great power to fine-tune a world for people like you and me. Perfection accounts for the self-sufficiency of the foundation: a foundation that is not self-sufficient is not perfect, while a perfect foundation is self-sufficient. Every positive attribute flows from the foundation's perfect nature.

Perfection also unifies the world. The world includes diverse dimensions: (1) mental, (2) material, (3) moral, and (4) mathematical. Why do these dimensions populate our world? Here is why. These diverse dimensions all flow from a single root: they flow from pure perfection in the foundation. From pure perfection flows the perfect way of being, which is the foundation of all moral principles. From pure perfection flows perfect knowledge, which is the foundation of all principles of reason and mathematics. Moreover, a perfect mind has every reason to create a material world suitable for other minds. The perfection of the foundation, then, successfully predicts every dimension of our world.

THE GREATEST POSSIBLE TREASURE

The bridge is now complete. All the steps are in place. We have an archway of lights shining into the deepest aspects of the foundation of reality. We have now arrived at the greatest possible treasure. Here, at the foundation of everything, we find the maximal concentration of goodness, value, and power imaginable. We find the *greatest reality imaginable*. And this reality we may call "God."[7]

By the light of reason, we can see what this God is *not*. This God is not a limited being, like the Zeus on Mount Olympus. This God is not an arbitrary flying spaghetti monster at the edges of the universe. This God is not the product of primitive superstition. This God is not the mere projection of our deepest desires. This God is not reducible to the postulate of someone's religion. This God is not hiding in the gaps

[7]See Aquinas, *Summa* I.2.

of our scientific knowledge. This God is not a being reachable only by a leap of blind faith.[8] These limited concepts of "God" block sight of a greater treasure. This treasure is the God revealed by reason. This God is perfect. This God is before all things that have been made. Without this God, there is nothing: no math, no logic, and no reason to produce other minds. The God of reason frees your mind so that you may discover the true greatness of the foundation of everything. God is as natural and untamed as reason itself.

God has the following attributes (as we have deduced):

1. God is self-sufficient.
2. God is independent.
3. God is necessarily existent.
4. God is ultimate.
5. God is eternally powerful.
6. God is purely actual (without gaps, holes, spots, blips, boundaries, wrinkles, or arbitrary limits).
7. God is unlimited.
8. God is the foundation of mind.
9. God is the foundation of matter.
10. God is the foundation of morals.
11. God is the foundation of math.
12. God is the foundation of reason.
13. God is purely positive.
14. God is maximally powerful.
15. God is maximally knowledgeable.
16. God is maximally good.
17. God is perfect.

Our bridge of reason has led us to the greatest God imaginable.

[8]R. Dawkins, *The God Delusion* (New York: Houghton Mifflin, 2006) targets many of these limited concepts of God.

SUMMARY

We can now summarize the entire argument of this book. The whole argument boils down to the following simple form:

Premise 1. Reality in total is self-sufficient (with no outside cause or explanation).

Premise 2. Nothing can be self-sufficient without a perfect foundation.

Conclusion. Therefore, reality has a perfect foundation.

Reason fills in supports for the premises. To support premise 1, reason reveals that nothing exists beyond the totality of all things. This means the totality of reality is self-sufficient.

Next, to support premise 2, reason reveals—from multiple angles—that any self-sufficient totality must have a perfect foundation. For an *imperfect* foundation generates two problems: (1) the problem of arbitrary limits and (2) the problem of construction.

The first problem is internal to the foundation itself. A merely imperfect foundation would have arbitrary limits. Limits not only add unnecessary complexity, they are not self-sufficient. By the uniformity of explanation, all limits alike have an explanation beyond themselves. Therefore, the foundation of all limits has no arbitrary limits—and so no arbitrary limit in value. The foundation can only be perfect (i.e., supremely valuable).

Second, without a perfect foundation, we have construction problems. An imperfect foundation lacks the materials for constructing the rest of reality. The rest of reality includes minds, matter, morals, and reasoning. A foundation of these things must, then, include the resources to produce these things. By the light of reason, only a perfect mental and moral nature includes the resources to construct the mental and moral dimensions of our world. Therefore, the foundation has a perfect mental and moral nature.

I will close this chapter by pointing to a picture that summarizes every element of every argument in this book. It is a picture of you. Within you are the materials for the bridge of reason. Your very existence verifies the first step on the bridge: something exists. You are not just *any* something. Within you are many treasures: thoughts, feelings, emotions, material complexity (to the extreme), moral sensations, mathematical insights, and the light of reason. The light of reason itself highlights a foundation for all these treasures within you.

By the light of reason, the foundation of all existence is the foundation of all the treasures within you. By reason, you can see that the basis of your thoughts is not a chaos of non-thoughts. The basis of your senses is not nonsense. The basis of the reasoning within you is not reasonless motions. By the light of reason, you can see that reason itself is the light within the foundation. By this light, the foundation can fashion a world with organization, purpose, and flowers. By this light, the foundation can anchor the moral landscape and paint the moral textures of your heart. By this light, the foundation can fine-tune a world for kingly creatures, like you.

CHAPTER 12

CHALLENGING THE BRIDGE

The bridge of reason leads to a great treasure, but is this treasure too good to be true? You might worry that while God's existence may make sense of certain things, it does not make sense of the whole picture of reality. During my own time of doubt, even after I discovered reasons to think God is real, arguments against God's existence also weighed in the balance. Could a supreme foundation fit with everything we see?

To help us think about this question, I will devote the next couple chapters to the examination of reasons to think the world does not have a supreme foundation. I will pay special attention to the problems that I have personally found the most perplexing. In this chapter, I will focus on evil and suffering, and then in the next I will examine a series of barriers related to other more specific concerns, such as about hell, religious diversity, and God's silence.

In this chapter, then, I begin with this question: why does evil exist? If the foundation of everything is perfect, how can any *bad* things exist in our world? How can perfection and imperfection co-exist? Questions like these can inspire us to question the integrity of our entire bridge.

This chapter is an introduction to a vast topic. Rather than attempt to solve every relevant problem, I will offer some instruments you can use for deeper analysis. These instruments have helped me to see the problems of life in a greater light.

ASSESSING POSSIBILITY

I will begin with possibility: is it even *possible* for perfection and imperfection to co-exist?

Here is a reason to think not. A perfect foundation cannot produce anything less than perfect. For example, maybe God could only create *perfect* flowers or *perfect* animals. Yet God would not allow anything bad to befall any of the created things. So, God and bad cannot co-exist.

The above reasoning points us to a classic argument from evil:

Premise 1. If God exists, then evil cannot exist.

Premise 2. Evil exists.

Conclusion. Therefore, God does not exist.

Philosophers call this argument the "logical" problem of evil.[1] They call it "logical" because logic alone is supposed to deliver the premise that God and evil cannot co-exist. The problem, then, is that evil *exists.* Therefore, God *does not.*

Does this argument succeed? Are the premises *true*?

Let us have a closer look at premise 1: if God exists, then evil cannot exist. This premise comes from the thought that God would prevent all the evil. Initially, we might think we can deduce what God *would* do from the definition of God's nature. God is perfectly *good* by definition. Therefore, by definition, God would have good reasons to prevent all evil.

However, in order for it to be true that God would prevent all evil, it must also be true that God couldn't have any *good reason* to allow evil. Imagine, though, that God sees certain goods that are only achievable if some evil is possible. Then those goods might give God good reason to allow some evil. Can we see that God *doesn't see* such goods? How?

The challenge here is to show that God *cannot* have a good reason for allowing evil. According to the purely logical argument from evil, we should be able to show—by reason—that God and evil are incompatible. Can we show that? The hypothesis that God allows evil for some good reason is not *itself* a contradiction (of the form A and not A). But can we tease out a hidden contradiction?

---

[1]J. L. Mackie, "Evil and Omnipotence," *Mind* LXIV, no. 254 (1955): 200-212 develops a version of this argument.

To my knowledge, no one has teased out a contradiction.[2] As a result, philosophers who specialize on the problem of evil (theists and atheists alike) have mostly moved away from the purely logical problem of evil.[3]

But let us look closer.

A GREAT STORY

You might worry that I am moving too quickly. Even if God and evil are not *explicitly* contradictory, they might still be impossible neighbors. Why *wouldn't* a perfectly good God prevent everything bad?

I want to proceed carefully. Instead of rushing past a real concern, I want to seek genuine insight leading to truth. Toward that end, let us consider more carefully whether God could allow evil *for some reason.* What reason could that possibly be?

To help us think about possible reasons for evil, I will tell two stories. Then I will consider their advantages and disadvantages to see which story God might prefer.

Here is the first story: God is alone and does nothing, forever. That's it. The end.

The second story includes more action. Imagine now that God causes a world to unfold to provide a place for a variety of beings to live. In this dynamic world, God gives some beings some freedom to design their own lives. They are kingly creatures. They have some freedom to develop their own stories.

So, which story might God prefer? Imagine God has a choice: either produce a diverse world with diverse beings, including kingly beings, *or* produce a world with no kingly beings. Which might God prefer?

To help us think about which option is best, let us consider the implications of both options. Start with the option that God creates a world without any kingly creatures. In that case, no creatures have ownership of their actions. No creatures enjoy the experience of designing any element of their own life. Instead, if any creatures exist, forces

---

[2]A. Plantinga, *Nature of Necessity* (New York: Oxford University Press, 1974) exposes a challenge with deducing a contradiction between God and evil by presenting a logically coherent reason God could have for allowing evil.

[3]That is what I hear at conferences and in conversations: they say we have no purely logical proof that God and evil cannot co-exist.

beyond their control pull the strings on all their actions. If someone decides to love someone, for example, that love is not up *to the creature*. Creatures have no freedom to rule to any extent (ever). Instead, their actions are ultimately and completely up to the forces that made the creature. Creatures are then subjects forced to serve God's nature.

Now think again about the other option: God creates a world with kingly creatures. Then what? Then creatures have a special opportunity. They have the opportunity to govern their own lives (at least to some extent). Creatures then have some freedom to rule. This freedom allows creatures to be more like God—that is, authors of their own pursuits. The creatures are kingly.[4]

The downside of creating kingly creatures is risk. Kingly creatures might rule badly. That's the risk.

Could God make creatures without any risk of bad? Here is an idea. Maybe God could avoid the risk by *making* the creatures to do good all the time. Then everything would *be* good all the time. That would be nice.

Yet making creatures do good has a cost. The cost is freedom to rule.[5] Without the freedom, the creatures are not kingly. They cannot design their own lives. Instead, they are puppets of God's demands. Would God want that?

To see what God might want, consider the costs and benefits. One benefit is that kingly creatures have some say in how their lives go. They have some freedom. With freedom, though, comes both responsibility and risk. If God creates kingly creatures, God risks a broken kingdom. The risk is a cost.

---

[4]Wes Morriston asks how the freedom to do evil could be good if God lacks that freedom, and my answer is that this freedom for creatures makes possible unforced relationships between kingly beings. See Morriston, "What Is So Good about Moral Freedom," *Philosophical Quarterly* 50 (2000): 344-358. See my reply, "On the Value of the Freedom to Do Evil," *Faith and Philosophy* 30 (2013): 418-428.

[5]Some philosophers think freedom implies alternative possibilities (imagine a fork in the road), while others say freedom does not imply alternative possibilities. We can leave this debate to the side for our purposes. My notion of freedom here is minimal. To be free requires only that *you* make some of your decisions, without anything *else* directly making you do what you do (such as forces of physics or God's hand). Philosophers sometimes call this the "source" condition on freedom. For the sake of modesty and inclusivity, I say only that something is special about a world with beings who are an original *source* of some of their actions.

Could the risk be worth it? Here is a reason to think this particular risk *might* be worth it. A broken kingdom, though tragic, can provide soil for many good things. In a broken world, heroes are born. Out of trouble, people can rise up to display great courage, compassion, and sacrificial love. That's not all: some of the most profound and special relationships spring from tough soil.

Let me be clear: I am not saying fruits of evil would *justify* evil. I don't think anything justifies evil. My thought, rather, is that even though the good doesn't erase the bad, God could take into account the potential good when considering the risks associated with making kingly creatures.

To investigate the potential reasons God might have for making kingly creatures, let us look closer at the elements of a good world. A good world is like a good *story*. What makes a story good? Here are some elements of a good story: adventure, exploration, progress, heroism, comic relief, courage in the face of uncertainty, layers of discovery, sacrifice, cleverness, good and evil, danger, victory, sub-plots, consistent rules that cannot be broken at the characters' whims, unpredictable surprises, a variety of dynamic characters, episodes that contribute to a larger plot, romance, hints of the future, tension, and release. A truly great story may involve a great sacrifice of love by the greatest character in that story.

Notice that our favorite stories include bad things in them. Tragedy may occur, yet all tragedies for all souls may be transformable into something beautiful and unexpected, perhaps in later scenes. All bad scenes could be *temporary*, while souls could reap jewels of value, wisdom, and love that may endure forever.

A good story could also have mysteries. The noblest characters in a good story could have trials where they do not see that the story is good. They may not understand how everything in their story could fit together. Still, even in times of uncertainty, the stories are not over. Future scenes can bring light to previous scenes. A great story includes layers of mystery to be uncovered and discovered.

Interestingly, our world has many elements of a grand story. Our world has many scenes and many characters.

Perhaps the author of the world is a coauthor, with us, of a grand story. Perhaps creatures can participate in the making of the world. The author then aims to work every problem and pain for greater good. The more intense the bad, the more intense the opportunities for intense good.

Here is a clue. When people die, some of them have a classic near-death experience, where they sense leaving their body. They sometimes report seeing a "being of light." In some cases, they say they asked this being questions, including questions about evil and suffering. I have heard many such reports, and all of them share a core message: *life is part of a far greater purpose*. Whether or not you believe any of these reports, my observation here is just that this message of a greater purpose *fits* the "great story" hypothesis.

For the sake of modesty, I offer a mere *hypothesis*:

Upside Hypothesis: God has fashioned a world for kingly beings (creatures with moral freedom), and God acts in orderly ways to work everything—including every bad event—together for as much long-term good as possible.

According to the Upside Hypothesis, God is always working to draw out the most good. While these creatures may sometimes rule very badly, God always works to draw out good from the bad. For example, God works to build souls who experience mercy and new hope, who discover what it is like to be heroes for others, who learn to love when it is hard, who understand forgiveness, who can work with others—and God—to restore a broken kingdom, and so on.

If the Upside Hypothesis is true, then all pains could be temporary, while good effects etched into souls could be everlasting. This hypothesis predicts a potential upside for every bad.

To be clear, I am not proposing that the original author of the world *causes* bad things just for the sake of a good story. Rather, the hypothesis is that the author creates a world for heroes and kingly creatures. If evil occurs, God is prepared to work bad things together for good.

Is the Upside Hypothesis *possible*? To answer this question, I take up the instrument of reason. Here is how things appear to me. When I peer into the Upside Hypothesis, I do not *see*—by any light of reason—that the Upside Hypothesis *cannot* be true. I do not see that a perfection foundation *must*—by the forces of logic—prevent all bad or create nothing at all.

On the contrary, *by the bridge of reason*, the ultimate foundation of things must be perfect. Full disclosure: I actually think I see clearly that a perfect being would in fact have good reason to create a world in which the Upside Hypothesis is true. An upside world is just the sort of reality I would expect from God.

My reason is simple: the Upside Hypothesis predicts great goods that are missing in a world that has no potential for bad. These goods include a diversity of everlasting souls and unending opportunities for growth, adventure, discovery, knowledge of reconciliation, relationships knitted by forgiveness, the many fruits of perseverance, unforced love, the experience of getting up again to discover the deepest treasures you had hoped for, conflict resolutions that lead to new beginnings, and so on. I would expect such goods from a good foundation.

The Upside Hypothesis is so good, actually, we might think it is *too good* to be true. Sure, it may be *possible*. But is it plausible?

To investigate whether the Upside Hypothesis might actually be true, we will need to consider the *probability* of the Upside Hypothesis. I turn to probability next.

ASSESSING PROBABILITY

A few years ago, I had a dream I was talking with a man about the problem of evil. This man's head was unusually large. He spoke with a strong voice as he explained to me that God would not allow the kinds of suffering we find in our world. The feeling I got from his voice was that he admired people who were honest about the world. He wanted people to face the facts.

I stood up to reply. I began to articulate a cold calculation. I felt conviction as I spoke about a great irony. "It is ironic," I said, "that you think evil is evidence against God." I went on to explain why I thought evil is actually evidence *for God*.

Here was the argument I gave in my dream. First, the mind of a perfect foundation is infinite: God's mind takes into account an infinite array of values and circumstances. God's mind goes beyond our minds. We cannot even fathom all the elements within God's mind. It follows, *by logic*, that we should expect that if God exists, God will have reasons for doing things we don't yet know about. Some reasons will be beyond our comprehension. On the other hand, if God doesn't exist, then we shouldn't even be talking here—nobody would exist.

As I delivered my argument, the man turned his head. What I saw next horrified me. One third of his head was gone. I could see his brain, red and flat.

The man then reached out his arm. I now saw he was missing a hand. He had a metal stump. He whispered that he lost his hand in a war. Then, as he reached to me, his face spoke without words. I felt an emotion from him say, "I want to feel your compassion."

Then I woke up.

As I lay in bed, two thoughts leaped into my mind. First, it occurred to me that the man's head injury made it difficult for him to think rationally. Second, I realized the man's greatest need was to feel valued. Perhaps the way for him to see God's goodness was not primarily through argument but through love.

In my dream, I encountered an important truth: the problem of evil touches the whole person. It does not *merely* touch the mind. I can offer a cold calculation of the probability, but a cold calculation is not medicine for a hurting heart.

We feel the problem of evil in the center of our hearts. In our center, we sense the badness of broken lives. In our center, we sense the reality of evil. In our center, we sense the seeds that sprout arguments in our minds.

Nevertheless, the mind and the heart can work together. The heart reveals the reality of evil. Meanwhile, the mind can help us assess the logical implications of evil.

To analyze the implications of evil, I take up once again the instrument of reason. With reason in hand, we can separate the clear from the unclear. The clearest path to truth starts with what is clear rather than what is unclear.

What is clear here? Is it *clear* that God would probably not have a good reason for allowing all the bad things that happen? To my mind, it is *unclear* what every reason could be. I *see* that I *don't see* every reason. What follows?

To figure out what follows, we can use the tool of "if-then" expectation—also known as conditional probability. For example, what do you expect *if* the foundation is perfect? What do you expect if it is not?

For the sake of challenge, let us consider the most troublesome cases of evil. These cases contain evil so bad and so hard to explain that no human has any idea what reason a perfectly good being could have for allowing them. Call these "mysterious" evils.

The tool of "if-then" expectation can help you analyze the mysterious evils from your own unique perspective. Simply ask yourself two questions:

Q1: How likely (*expected*) are mysterious evils *if* God exists?

Q2: How likely (*expected*) are mysterious evils *if* God does not exist?

Start with Q1: would you expect mysterious evils *if* God exists? Since I cannot answer this question for you without having your life experiences, I will simply share my own analysis to illustrate the "if-then" tool. You can consider the matter from your perspective.

So, here is how things seem to me. *If* God exists, then the Upside Hypothesis—where all things work together for good—is precisely what I would expect to be true. Specifically, I would expect the goods of a grand story. I would expect the usual elements of a grand story, including scenes suited for heroes, and episodes of uncertainty.

Moreover, I would expect coauthors of a real story. I would expect to find kingly characters who can help decide how things unfold. And, if things unfold poorly, I would indeed expect the ultimate author to help work bad things for good.

I would also expect some of God's reasons to be above my current knowledge. Sure, I would expect to understand at least *some* of God's reasons. But I certainly would not expect to see all of them. For I would expect God's maximal mind to include ideas I have not yet considered.

Therefore, on reflection, my own answer to Q1 is this: the likelihood of at least some mysterious evils if God exists is *not low*.

Going Deeper

To be sure, some kinds of evil are indeed unlikely if God exists. For example, Sue stubs her right toe at 2:03 p.m. EST on a rock outside my house. That isn't likely if God exists.

But, of course, the event just mentioned isn't likely if God *doesn't exist*, either. So it is not relevant to our inquiry. The relevant categories, then, are more general. In this chapter, I am focusing on three of the most general categories: (1) evil in general, (2) moral evil, and (3) mysterious evil. In the next chapter, I will focus on additional categories (including natural evil, divine hiddenness, and others).

Now for Q2: how likely are mysterious evils *without* God's existence? Here is how things seem to me. If God does not exist, then it is unexpected that any evil would exist. For example, without a good, powerful, and wise foundation, it is less likely—I'd say *impossible*—for the things to be finely-tuned for people, consciousness, and morality. These things are prerequisites for any bad to exist. So, without a good, powerful, and wise foundation, I would not expect any bad to exist.

The bridge of reason reinforces this analysis. The materials from previous chapters (i.e., about the foundation of minds, matter, morals, and reason) reduce the probability of evil without God down to zero in my mind (or near zero).

From these answers, I can then deduce the following result: it is more likely—more expected—that some mysterious evils would exist *if* God exists than if God does not exist. Again, the existence of some mystery is expected on the Upside Hypothesis, and the Upside Hypothesis is expected on God's existence. By contrast, without God's existence, I don't think it is even possible, let alone probable, for any moral communities to exist—and without moral communities, moral mysteries are impossible. My cold calculation reveals to my mind, then, that I should actually expect to find mysterious evils if God *does* exist. In other words, by this analysis, the existence of mysterious evils makes the most sense only if God exists.

I have given you my own analysis. I invite you to consider the "if-then" expectations from your own perspective. See what you see.

Going Deeper

You might wonder how I could say that mysterious evils point to God's existence when the problem of evil is supposed to be a problem for God's existence. How can the same evils that point away from God's existence also point to God's existence?

Here is my answer. I actually think that the standard "evidence"-based arguments from mysterious evil against God arise from two tempting mistakes. I'll explain.

Mistake 1: Selection-effect. The mistake here is to select out a sample of events that stack the deck in one direction. For example, we could select out a whole bunch of particular mysterious evils. By definition, no known reason makes sense of them. It may then be tempting to infer that probably no *actual* reason makes sense of them.[6]

This inference is a mistake, however. It is like inferring that probably no houses exist in Detroit from the fact that Detroit has empty lots. Yes, if we focus only on the empty lots, those lots might suggest that the whole city is empty. However, in a large enough city, we can *expect* to find many empty lots. So finding empty lots is not by itself good evidence that the entire city is empty.

In the same way, in a large enough world crafted by a large enough mind, we can expect to find many mysterious events. If all the events were mysterious, that may indeed be a problem—like finding that every lot in Detroit is empty. But that's not what we find. More to the point, finding empty lots is not by itself good evidence that the entire city is empty.[7]

Mistake 2: Not seeing versus seeing not. I do *not* see any spiders in my neighborhood, but it would be a mistake to infer that I do see the absence of all spiders in my neighborhood. Similarly, I do *not* see the reason for mysterious evil (by definition). But it would be a mistake to infer that I *do* see the absence of all God's reasons.[8] Not seeing is not the same as seeing not.

---

[6]Cf. M. Tooley, "The Problem of Evil," *Stanford Encyclopedia of Philosophy* (2015), https://plato.stanford.edu/entries/evil/.

[7]Cf. T. Dougherty and A. Pruss, "Evil and the Problem of Anomaly," *Oxford Studies in Philosophy of Religion* 5 (2014): 49-87.

[8]S. Wykstra, "Rowe's Noseeum Arguments from Evil," in *The Evidential Argument from Evil*, ed. D. Howard-Snyder, 126-50 (Bloomington: Indiana University Press, 1996) calls this inference "the noseeum inference."

Seeing this difference protects us from error. To illustrate, suppose I infer from my lack of seeing spiders that, probably, no spiders exist. That inference is a mistake because if my neighborhood did have some spiders (and surely it does), I would not thereby expect to see a spider right now. My neighborhood is large, after all, while spiders are small and usually out of sight.

We can avoid a similar mistake when thinking about mysterious evils. Suppose I infer that probably God has no reason for evil from my own lack of seeing a reason. This inference is also a mistake because if God did have a reason, I would not thereby expect to see it right now. Maybe later.

Once we recognize these mistakes, we can avoid them. If we avoid them, then we are free to consider the problem of evil in a new light. Perhaps we will not rush to assume the problem of evil is a *problem* for the existence of God. By my analysis, the existence of mysterious evil, at least, is a problem for a mindless foundation, not for the existence of God.

The instruments of analysis I have offered certainly do not settle every question or calm every worry. You might wonder about specific categories of bad, such as viral infections, innocent victims of torture, shattered hopes, God's silence, and so on. Some of these categories may seem decidedly unexpected on God's existence. In an effort to gain greater clarity, therefore, I will offer some further thoughts in the next chapter on some of the most troubling categories of evil I have pondered. My aim is to encourage you using a tool of reason aimed at nothing but truth.

SUMMARY

Evil is a problem that threatens the integrity of our entire bridge of reason. Must our bridge collapse?

Reason helps us assess the implications of evil. With reason in hand, we can separate what is clear from what is unclear. It is clear that a perfect mind *could* have good reasons to create a morally interesting world, including a world with morally free, kingly beings. It is *not* clear, by contrast, that everyone would always know every reason a perfect mind might have for allowing evil. In fact, it is reasonable to think that great mysteries and great challenges are part of any great story.

CHAPTER 13

REMOVING BARRIERS

People from around the world sometimes email me questions about God. Some of their questions present obstacles to stepping onto this book's bridge of reason. They see orange cones warning them to stay off any bridge that leads to such a great treasure.

In this chapter, I will address eight of the most common and challenging questions. While each question deserves a book in its own right (and many qualified books exist),[1] my goal here is modest: I want to show how, by the light of reason, I personally walk past the orange cones. My method, again, is to separate what is *clear* from what is *unclear*.

EIGHT BARRIERS TO BELIEF

Barrier 1. Believers in God fail to base their beliefs on good evidence. Instead, the root of their belief is faith and hope, not sight.

The problem is worse for smart believers: smart believers *rationalize* their beliefs. They want to believe so badly they find an argument to support their hope. They fear death. They long for purpose. They find the reasons to nourish their heart. Their beliefs grow from invisible roots inside.

[1]Just to name a few that I've personally found helpful: C. S. Lewis, *The Problem of Pain* (New York: Harper Collins, 1940); A. Plantinga, *Nature of Necessity* (New York: Oxford University Press, 1974); R. Swinburne, *Providence and the Problem of Evil* (Oxford: Clarendon, 1998); P. van Inwagen, *The Problem of Evil* (Oxford: Oxford University Press, 2006); and T. Dougherty, *The Problem of Animal Pain: A Theodicy for All Creatures Great and Small* (New York: Palgrave, 2014).

A smart person who wants to believe in God might be able to create a bridge of reason to get there. Let us not fool ourselves, though. Let us have the courage to face reality as it is.

Reflection. This first barrier may be the most common of them all, and it reflects virtue, courage, and honesty.

The worry is legitimate. On the one side, we have careful skeptics. They seek evidence. They seek truth. They see the value of science. On the other side, we have the believers. If believers are dogmatic, intellectually dishonest, and judgmental while the skeptics are careful truth-seekers, then whose side is more credible? Whose side do we want to be on?

I want to join the skeptics.

I offer for your consideration a distinction between two types of faith. We can separate blind faith from a "faith that sees." While blind faith comes with many vices, I'd like to draw attention to another faith—a courage—that is based on *sight*.

Blind faith looks like this. You are eyeing a stock chart of a small oil company. You notice that the price of the stock has nearly doubled over the last month. You think it might continue to rise, but you do not know much of anything about the company or about the market. You keep watching the stock each day. It keeps rising. You worry you are missing out. So one morning, you log into your brokerage account, and you decide to buy as many shares of this company as you can. You put your entire emergency fund into this stock, as you tell yourself, "This stock will rise high." You have put your faith in this stock. Sorry, wife.

The next day, you see that gas prices have dropped. And you hear on the radio that oil prices *might* be about to fall. The world is ambiguous. Yet in your mind, you form a picture of your stock rising, and you decide to focus on this picture. When you return home, you check a few stats online and find a sea of conflicting information about oil prices. You keep in your mind the picture of a rising stock, and your eyes gravitate toward a few stats that support your picture. You continue to have faith that the stock will rise.

I hear many advertisements for blind faith. It is a virtue, they say, to believe when you *don't* see. It stretches you. It takes courage. Some say it is the only way to be "saved."

Yet my skeptical friends are right: *blind faith is a leap into the dark.* Blind faith does not flow from evidence. Rather, it flows from fear or a wish. Blind leapers do not *test* whether they will land somewhere safe. Blind leapers may get lucky; they land upon a treasure by chance. Without sight, however, blind leapers are gamblers who more often fall into the pits. And they lead others to fall with them.

During my time of doubt, the advertisements I heard for blind leaping reinforced my worries. Is their belief in God rooted ultimately in a desire to protect previous beliefs? I couldn't trust blind leapers over truth testers. How could I?

Blindness is not the only fuel for faith, however. I found a starkly different fuel. This fuel is sight-based. Its central ingredient is *evidence.* (At this point, some readers may not want to call the thing I'm talking about "faith," and that is fine. Call it what you like.)

To illustrate the "faith" I have in mind, suppose your best friend tells you that he has sent you a gift in the mail. You do not presently see the gift. Yet you expect—*trust*—you'll be receiving a package soon. Your expectation comes from your prior knowledge of your friend and of the world. It comes from sight.

Sight-based faith often takes both courage and discipline. For example, it took courage for me to get on an airplane to return to the United States from Cambodia. I was extremely jet lagged, and I felt afraid of falling into the ocean. Very afraid. I knew my fear had no fact. Yet I felt within my mind a gravitational pull to focus on the waves. I had to decide to focus on the facts about flight safety, and I had to decide to step on the plane.

It can take discipline to *focus* on the facts rather than on the waves. Planes are not 100 percent reliable, and I knew that. I also knew that my fear far outmatched the level of risk. Sometimes it takes courage to trust the facts.

Sight-based faith leads to rewards. Athletes who focus on their potential prize are keeping in view an inspiring, sight-based reason to push forward. Sight-based faith is a powerful force that allows people to obtain many treasures, including victories, inventions, relationships, and new discoveries. It takes wisdom and virtue to be skeptical of things you should be skeptical of, while *also* straining to see good truths.

I hope it is clear that when I use the term *sight*, I do not merely mean sight with your eyes. I mean more broadly awareness through any sense. Your memory sense, for example, supplies you with evidence of things you did earlier today. Additionally, you can see truths about logic using your sense of reason. And so on. You can "see" in many ways.

Sight-based faith is often possible even when there is a conflict, or lack of concord, between multiple sources of sight. For example, my wife tells me that she will pick me up at the airport. I stand by the curb, waiting. My eyes lack the anticipated stimulation from photons: I don't see her here. However, I focus my attention on memories of our history together. Those memories give me ample reason to trust that she will likely arrive soon. A few more minutes elapse. There she comes! I am happy but not surprised.

I do not mean to suggest that there are never times to take a risk or that everyone is in the same position to trust the same things. Sometimes a little leaping may be worth a little risk, such as when you estimate that the odds are in your favor. Other times not. It takes wisdom to know when a risk is worth it, and *you* are the best person to assess what you think you see, from your perspective.

I would like to close by distinguishing *sight* from *hope*. Before you see, you can carry hope. Hope is a flashlight that can lead to greater sight. While greed inspires a leap into darkness, honest hope inspires more light on a subject. The reward is greater understanding and genuine sight. Sometimes you even discover treasure.

Barrier 2. Some people have theorized that the "perfect" foundation is perfectly good. But why think that? Maybe the foundation is perfectly bad.

Response. The materials of our bridge support the following answer: good and bad are *asymmetric* (see chapter nine). For example, if I destroy someone's face, my act is bad precisely because I've destroyed something *good*. Without something good already in place, there cannot be any badness.

Consider, moreover, that there can only be a distinction between good and bad if there is some moral standard that distinguishes between good actions and bad actions.[2] Such a standard is itself good. For this

---

[2]Cf. C. S. Lewis, *Mere Christianity* (New York: Harper Collins, 1952), 3-34.

reason, if there is any bad at all, then there is already a prior good in place. This good lies ultimately in the foundation of everything. If the foundation has some good, then it must be *purely* and *completely* good (by the arguments against arbitrary limits). I conclude, therefore, that the foundation of reality cannot be bad. Reason won't allow it.

Barrier 3. If God uses bad for greater good, then why should *we* prevent the bad? Why should we get in the way of God's plan?

To illustrate the problem, suppose you see a child about to run out onto a busy street. You would surely try to stop the child, right? But then why doesn't *God*? Is the answer that God will use every harm for a greater good? But if that's the answer, then to prevent harm is to prevent a *greater good*. So why should *we* prevent any harm?

Response. This barrier is valuable because it can help deter us away from a certain faulty view of God. Allow me to explain.

The faulty view, in my opinion, is that God wants each harm to happen. On this view, every harm is a puzzle piece in God's perfect, grand plan. If any harmful piece were missing, the total picture would be less than perfect.

The problem I have with the "perfect picture" theory is that it seems to me to remove *our responsibility*. We would then have no say about anything. After all, every event would be *necessary* for God's total picture.

Here is a different picture. Imagine God creates a world with kingly creatures. These creatures can be *coauthors* of the real story.

This picture entails, by reason, a certain risk. If God makes kingly creatures, God must limit himself in a certain way: while God *could* prevent every bad choice, doing so would effectively remove all kingly natures. It follows, therefore, that in order to create a world with responsible (kingly) creatures, God is constrained—by reason itself—to leave some things in the hands of the creatures.

To illustrate, suppose I decide to prevent a child from running into a busy street. Then the relationship that I forge and the heroism I display are great goods. These goods are within *my* responsibility. No one, not even God, can make a kingly creature live up to their responsibility.

On this picture, God has a responsibility we do not have. In particular, God is responsible for the *basic rules* of the whole picture; we aren't. If God wants kingly creatures to exist, then God must create rules consistent with the existence of kingly creatures. It is not that God makes the whole picture. Rather, God makes it so that we can help make the picture.

Here is the crucial point: even while God can work all bad for far greater good, the *greatest* goods may come from kingly creatures who, in their independence, choose to take responsibility.

To be clear, this "kingly creatures" answer does not solve every problem or explain every evil. There are more problems to consider. My purpose here is merely to separate one particular problem from others. The problem at hand is about responsibility: why should we do our responsibility *if* God would use our failures for good anyway? My answer is this: we get to be coauthors of a great picture; if God forced our every move, we would not be kingly creatures.

Barrier 4. How could God send people to hell? Imagine your neighbor says he'll torture you if you don't love him. That neighbor is not good. How, then, could God be good if God tortures creatures who don't love God?

Response. Since my purpose is to follow reason where it leads, let us consider where reason leads here.

To begin, reason removes contradictory accounts of God's justice. Suppose a certain account of hell contradicts perfect goodness. Then, since God's nature includes the standard of perfect goodness and justice, an *unjust* account of hell cannot be correct. Rather than infer that a perfect foundation cannot exist, reason takes us in the other direction: any concept of hell that is incompatible with perfect goodness must be mistaken.

The result of reason can then bring us comfort. Whatever the correct theory of the world, it must be compatible with supreme goodness—if indeed supreme goodness is in the nature of the foundation.

Now to be clear, I am not *assuming* every account of hell must contradict supreme goodness. It is a further question whether a theory of hell could make sense. For the sake of exploration, then, let us have a closer look at what reason might reveal about hell.

Start with God. By reason, a perfect foundation (God) *must have* a perfect nature. By God's perfect nature, God must be good. Hence, God is not good by first making a series of choices. Rather, God includes the ultimate standard of goodness. God's nature, therefore, includes the ultimate moral bar. The standard of goodness is part of the fabric of the foundation's perfect nature.

What follows? This: anyone who separates from goodness thereby—of necessity—separates from the nature of God. To separate oneself from God *is* to separate oneself from goodness, and vice versa.

In view of this connection between God and goodness, we could actually define "hell" in terms of separation from God. The idea, then, is that the more we are separate from true *goodness* (in all its forms), the more we experience the consequences of that separation—such as shame, injustice, turmoil, and so on. The experience of these consequences, whether in this life or the next, is the *pain of hell*. The pain of hell, by this definition, is the pain of separation from goodness.

Notice that on this account, we can experience "hell" right now. We can be separate from goodness right now (whether by our own doing or the doing of others), and we can feel that separation.

It is an axiom of goodness that separation from goodness is not good. This axiom is not a consequence of God's choice. Rather, it is a consequence of reason itself.

By reason, then, hell (as separation from goodness) is not a place that God simply *decides* to push people into. Many people think of hell as a prison, like Alcatraz, which God could, if God wanted to, abolish. But if hell is separation from goodness, then God could no more get rid of "hell" than God could get rid of goodness itself, unless God abolishes all kingly creatures. Hell, as separation from goodness, has its negative aspects, not by God's desire, but by what it means to be separate from goodness.

From here, we can see how God is importantly different from your neighbor. God includes the ultimate standard of goodness, while your neighbor does not. If you separate yourself from your neighbor, you do not thereby separate yourself from the standard of goodness. Your neighbor is not the ultimate standard of goodness. By contrast, if you separate yourself from the goodness within the nature of God, you thereby separate yourself from the standard of goodness.

So, then, what does reason tell us about "hell"? Reason does not tell us that hell is God's desire, God's act of vindication, or God's method of forcing people to love God with threats of violence. Rather, reason reveals the opposite of those things. While separation from goodness may be in the hands of kingly creatures, it is not in the heart of God.

To be clear, I am not suggesting *you* are to blame for experiencing a distance from goodness. There are many factors in play. Here I want to suggest to you, merely, that hell need not be an *obstacle* to God. If a form of hell is actually *incompatible* with God, then by reason, that form of hell does not exist. If, on the other hand, a form of hell is the pain of separation from goodness, then instead of keeping you from God, this pain could actually be an *invitation* to draw nearer to the fountain of all that is good, by the light you see most clearly within you.

You might wonder how the "separation" model fits with the particular accounts people give about the afterlife. Rather than wade through the many theories, I will point to three different accounts for your own assessment. These accounts can help you separate the clear from the unclear, from your own perspective.

Account 1. God creates kingly creatures who are capable of living apart from God's goodness. Those who willfully and persistently reject love and life (whether in this life or the next) live in a "hell" of their own making. Scholars who have helped me appreciate this view are C. S. Lewis and Jerry Walls.[3]

Account 2. Justice requires that people continue to experience consequences *for as long as they continue to do evil.* Hell (separation from goodness) lasts as long as evil lasts. If someone continues to do evil without end, then justice requires that their hell continue just as long. The scholar who first helped me appreciate this option was William Lane Craig.[4]

Account 3. The ultimate purpose of hell—and of all perfect punishment—is to *purify*. On this account, no soul stays in conscious torment endlessly. Scholars who have helped me appreciate this view are Thomas Talbot and Keith DeRose.[5]

---

[3]C. S. Lewis, *The Great Divorce* (New York: Harper Collins, 1946); and J. Walls, *Purgatory: The Logic of Total Transformation* (Oxford: Oxford University Press, 2012).

[4]W. L. Craig, "Can a Loving God Send People to Hell? The Craig-Bradley Debate," Simon Fraser University (1994), www.reasonablefaith.org/media/debates/can-a-loving-god-send-people-to-hell-the-craig-bradley-debate/.

[5]T. Talbott, *The Inescapable Love of God*, 2nd ed. (Eugene, OR: Cascade, 2014); and K. DeRose, "Universalism and the Bible," https://campuspress.yale.edu/keithderose/.

Ultimately, the safest path to truth is to step along what is *clear*, not what is *unclear*. Here is what reason makes clear to my mind: the perfect nature of a perfect foundation cannot be imperfect. By this clear step, I see that a perfectly good being cannot have imperfect rules of justice. Its rules must be perfect. I deduce the following conclusion: a perfectly good being will judge justly.

This result is a clear lens by which we may assess various reports about the hereafter.

Barrier 5. Why does God condemn people for being born in the wrong religion?

Response. My response is once again to separate what is clear from what is unclear. Rather than attempt to defend any clearly *unjust* account of justice, questions about religion invite me to consider what a perfectly just foundation would truly be like.

I'd like to share an idea that goes back to Jesus of Nazareth. Whatever you may think about this figure (even if you doubt he existed!), his name is associated with a certain fascinating story that has seeds for an answer I personally find deeply helpful. This answer is one you may not have heard in a church.

Here is the story (according to the book of Matthew):

> The King will say to those on his right, "Come, you who are blessed by my Father; take your inheritance, the kingdom prepared for you since the creation of the world. For I was hungry and you gave me something to eat, I was thirsty and you gave me something to drink, I was a stranger and you invited me in, I needed clothes and you clothed me, I was sick and you looked after me, I was in prison and you came to visit me."
>
> Then the righteous will answer him, "Lord, when did we see you hungry and feed you, or thirsty and give you something to drink? When did we see you a stranger and invite you in, or needing clothes and clothe you? When did we see you sick or in prison and go to visit you?"
>
> The King will reply, "Truly I tell you, whatever you did for one of the least of these brothers and sisters of mine, *you did for me*." (Matt 25:34-40, emphasis added)

Notice that the king—representing God—is interested in how we love people. By loving people, we love the king.

C. S. Lewis illustrates this same theme in his book *The Last Battle* (the seventh and final book of his *Chronicles of Narnia*). He describes a creature, Emeth, who serves the evil master, Tash. Emeth doesn't realize that Tash is evil. In the final scene, Emeth meets Aslan, who represents God. Emeth is worried because he had spent his entire life serving the enemy Tash. But Aslan tells Emeth that "all the service thou hast done to Tash, I account as service done to me."[6] He explains, "No service which is vile can be done to me, and none which is not vile can be done to him."[7] In other words, by loving people, *we love God*.

Here is another clue that points in the same direction. People who have near death experiences (NDEs) report the universal value of love. From all cultures, people come back with a common message: what matters most—the highest good—is that people *love people*.

To be clear, I am not proposing that we can "earn" our way to heaven just by loving people enough. I think *grace* is also part of the story. My suggestion, rather, is that God can give each person exactly what that person needs at the right times. God can make a truly good path available to you in the unique ways that make sense to you.

I propose, therefore, the following hypothesis (inspired by both reason and reports of revelation): *God looks at the heart*. God works with people according to their response to the light they have. As people respond well to their current light of understanding, God reveals more.

While I think this hypothesis is correct, as far as it goes, I'd like to make a more basic point about God's justice. My thought is this: the correct theory of God's perfect justice—*whatever it is*—must, by the light of reason, be compatible with perfect justice. That is most clear.

Barrier 6. How could God allow innocent people, especially kids, to suffer and die from diseases or natural disasters?

Response. This objection is about "natural" evil. Natural evil is the pain and suffering that results from natural events, like earthquakes,

---

[6]C. S. Lewis, *The Last Battle* (New York: Harper Collins, 1956), 188.
[7]Lewis, *Last Battle*, 189.

hurricanes, and floods. I have several connected thoughts to share about how to make sense of natural evil.

To start, a natural order has value. The natural order gives rise to great goods, creaturely growth and development, displays of sacrificial love, the overcoming of obstacles, and relationships knitted in the fabric of common trials. In the soil of trouble, heroes arise.

Next, God can aim at order without aiming at negative events that can happen within an orderly arena. For example, if an ocean wave tips over your boat, it does not mean God was pushing the wave along with the goal of tipping your boat. The foundation of reality can aim at order and its fruits without also aiming at unfortunate events within that order.

To illustrate, imagine the foundation of physical laws fashions arenas for diverse creatures. Some creatures live in the sea, while others live on the land. These arenas may include risks and rewards, which themselves can contribute to the growth of finite creatures along many lines. God can aim for growth without specifically aiming to cause any harm. (If this section were an entire book, I would also point out the potential benefits of having streams of randomness—or indeterminacy—in the natural order. I would explain how uncertainty, even for God, provides a context for many valuable experiences, including surprise, autonomous creation, anticipation, appreciation, and many others. Here it suffices to point to the possibility of greater value in a world that is not completely preprogramed.[8])

Another thought: all unfortunate byproducts of order can be temporary, while its results can reap value in everlasting souls. Every affliction, including every affliction caused by natural events, has the power to produce everlasting jewels of character, insight, and specially knitted love bonds. Temporary pains can reap unique and everlasting value.

Now to be clear, I am not suggesting that the value that emerges is God's *reason* for evil. I don't think God causes tears in order to build a kingdom. Rather, my thought is that God establishes orderly arenas for the many fruits that can spring up in a world with many kinds of creatures.

[8]For more on reasons for randomness, see J. Wessling and J. Rasmussen, "Reasons for Randomness," *Theology and Science* 13, no. 3 (2015): 288-304.

The arenas are good, but not completely tame. Danger is possible. Problems can happen. Unfairness can tip a boat. Disaster can strike.

Danger serves a purpose, though. The purpose of our world is not merely to sustain sheep. This world is an arena for heroes, problem-solvers, and kingly creatures. When the innocent suffer in this arena, their suffering is tragic, but their very sorrows achieve for them an everlasting value that far outweighs them all.

Another thought: we see only a fraction of every life story. We do not see every possible connection between every bad and every good for every creature. Here I think intellectual humility protects us from hasty inferences.

What is *clear* here? Is it clear that God has no good reasons or answers? Is it clear that a good foundation cannot, or will not, create an orderly world where natural disasters are possible? The light of reason makes none of those things clear to my mind.

Here is what reason makes clear. A perfectly good foundation *cannot be bad*. From this clear thing, I infer that a perfectly good foundation cannot work all things together for *bad*. Instead, a perfect foundation will work things together for good, including long-term and currently unseen good.

A perfect foundation has perfect sight of every possible good, while we do not. The trip to truth is safer when guided by clear (sight-based) steps than when guided by unclear (leap-based) steps. I recommend, therefore, that we follow the clear steps of reason rather than fall into a pit of darkness.

Barrier 7. Why doesn't God perform miracles today?

Ask God to write his name in the sky. It won't happen. God answers prayers in the same way as *an imaginary god would*—without detection.[9]

Response. A perfect foundation provides a lens for interpreting how God might interact with the world. We can expect that a perfect foundation of the universe would cause things to unfold in a *rational*—and therefore *orderly*—way. If the foundation of reality is indeed mind-like (see chapters seven through ten), then we can expect an

[9]Two popular websites that express this objection in popular terms are godisimaginary.com and whywontgodhealamputees.com. These websites challenge Christians to think critically about whether God does anything detectible.

orderly universe. Order is the mark of a mind: minds organize events, arrange paint into pictures, decree laws and regulations, and so on. On this framework, God's normal ways are "natural" because they are orderly, law-like, and predictable.

The natural order is itself good because it is foundational to productive science, creaturely growth, adventure, personal responsibility, and the forging of complex, diverse relationships and orderly societies. We can expect a perfect God, then, to make laws that give creatures opportunities to explore, grow, have adventures, encounter puzzles and perplexing questions, and be heroes in loving people. A good foundation predicts an orderly world.

To be clear, I am not suggesting that God *couldn't* act in unusual or unpredictable ways. Perhaps God could "break" certain laws for unique, special purposes—or because of higher laws.

My point is that if God exists *throughout* the universe (and not merely outside it), then we should expect order (laws) throughout the universe. God might sometimes act unusually. But that would be unusual! God doesn't regularly act irregularly. My proposal, then, is that God acts *through* nature—like a hand in a glove.

This "natural" God is fully consistent with scientific studies on prayer. In fact, some studies indicate a positive effect from prayer.[10] Moreover, some studies indicate a positive effect of mental behavior on biological function.[11]

The most common objection to these studies is that they do not rule out "natural" causes. Fair enough. My point, however, has been that natural causes are a *way* to answer prayer. This way of acting does not make God undetectable. The opposite is so: acting in orderly ways is the mark of a rational mind. After all, we should expect the foundation of the natural order to work through "natural" causes, since "natural causes" are the streams of order flowing from the foundation of all order. In other words, natural causes are the normal causes of a *rational mind* acting throughout the universe.

---

[10]See this meta-analysis by K. M. Masters and G. Spielmans, "Prayer and Health: Review, Meta-Analysis, and Research Agenda," *Journal of Behavioral Medicine* 30 (2007): 329-38.

[11]J. M. Shwartz and S. Begley, *The Mind and the Brain: Neuroplasticity and the Power of Mental Force* (New York: Harper Collins, 2002).

Here, then, is how prayer might work. Suppose I pray for you, and suppose my prayer sets off a natural chain of causes that moves from my thoughts to your physical or emotional well-being. Prayer could then work through natural laws.

Would it follow that *God* isn't involved in prayer? No. Quite the opposite: a perfect foundation predicts that God is involved everywhere. God is the foundation of the entire natural order. Natural "laws" are themselves sustained by God's rational thoughts.

Return with me to this important question: what is clear? Is it *clear* that a perfect foundation would act *unorderly* (breaking its "natural" laws) any time someone asks it to? Is it clear that irregular events would be regular, normal, everyday happenings? If anything is clear here, it is that irregular events *wouldn't* be regular.

So, why won't God heal amputees? Here is why: doing so, right when you ask God to do so, would destroy the natural order of reality. It would make God your puppet. Reason refuses this result.

Barrier 8. Why doesn't God make his existence more obvious to everyone?[12]

Response. When I first met my wife, Rachel, I fell in "*like*" with her right away. I walked up to her, my heart increasing its beat. I asked, "Would you like to get together some time to talk about . . . *philosophy*?"

She said, "Okay."

We met and had that philosophy talk, and many others. My like for her grew.

But I wondered, *Is her interest in me purely platonic?*

Without knowing whether she might like me as much as I liked her, I came up with the most ingenious idea. I devised a scavenger hunt that would ultimately lead to a marriage proposal! This idea soon gave birth to action, and I wrote notes and created puzzles. The notes led to other notes, and the puzzles and encoded messages led to more clues. The final clue was a coded message inviting Rachel on a date where I would propose to her. I laid these notes down before we ever started dating.

Eventually, she did find the first clue. Her curiosity was moderate. She didn't search much for the next clue. Meanwhile, our conversations

[12]The best scholarly articulation of this concern is in J. Schellenberg, *The Hiddenness Argument: Philosophy's New Challenge to Belief in God* (New York: Oxford University Press, 2015).

transformed into watching episodes of Stargate together. I still didn't know if she liked me or how much. She said nothing about her feelings. (Nor did I.)

Her curiosity grew. She began to search for the next clue in the scavenger hunt. As our relationship grew, her interest in searching for the clues increased.

Then, on June 3, 2007, she decoded the final clue. On this most interesting day, she joined me on a date. I bought her a dress and shoes, and I took her to a fancy dinner. During dinner, I spontaneously laughed out loud as I imagined what I was about to do.

Within minutes of my laugh, I invited Rachel for a short walk toward an outdoor archway. As we reached a place surrounded by flowers, I got on my knee and expressed my desire to marry her. Then, with heart pounding, I asked her if she wanted to be my wife.

She said, "Yes!" with tears coming down her cheeks. It was a most joyful day, from which thousands of joyful days have followed.

The point of this story is to bring into focus a question: why did I not tell Rachel how much I loved her *from the beginning*? Here is why. In my pursuit of her, I didn't want her to merely know that I loved her. I wanted her to *discover* my love for her. And I wanted her to discover it from her *own* interest. So I placed clues leading to other clues as a way of inviting her on an adventure leading to romance and further discovery.

The means of establishing our relationship enhances our current relationship together. We will never forget the excitement of discovering each other's affection.

This story inspires me to spot several reasons God might be less than entirely obvious to everyone at all times. Here are a few proposals:

First, there is value in *discovering* the deeper meaning and nature of God's love over time (longer periods of time for greater discoveries). Perhaps leaving a religion is part of the process of getting away from a concept of love that is too narrow, too exclusive, and too limited. Perhaps God would rather you experience the freedom from religion than to cling to a love that is tied to "us" vs. "them" ("in" vs. "out"). Perhaps your freedom to see a larger world (larger than *any* religion can comprehend) is ultimately a means to a deeper insight into the kind of true love that underlies the whole world.

Second, there is value in *seeking* treasures in the face of uncertainty.

Third, there is value in maintaining a natural order to the universe, despite certain temporary lacks that can sometimes result, including a lack of reasons to believe in a perfect foundation.

Fourth, some values affect creature-to-creature relationships. For example, a disagreement about God's reality, even if for a stage, creates opportunities for some of the most interesting and most beautiful expressions of respect for people who see the world differently. It is beautiful when people who have very different views of reality are nonetheless kind to each other, learn from each other, and genuinely love each other.

Fifth, a lack of seeing every treasure provides unique opportunities for service. People who discover treasures can serve others by helping them see something new and valuable—perhaps by building for them a bridge of reason.

Beyond all these things, reason reveals another reason for a lack of sight. God's love, if truly *real*, would have infinitely many layers of depth displayed in infinitely many forms. In view of God's infinite depth, our discovery of the depths and forms of God—of the ultimate foundation—may have no end. Perhaps, by the nature of growth, many good things, including good things about God, will come into view across episodes, different episodes for different people.

On some level, then, we are all skeptics; no one sees every treasure waiting for discovery. We need each other, from all perspectives, to see more good things in the foundation of all things.

I wish to emphasize that it is not necessarily someone's fault for not seeing a treasure. Rachel didn't know how much I liked her, but that wasn't her fault at all. In fact, it was my hope that she would discover that I liked her. I didn't blame her for not knowing more about me right away. Rather, I waited in eager anticipation.

SUMMARY

In this chapter, I have attempted to remove some of the orange cones that deter people from stepping on the bridge of reason. You may be aware of other barriers. I invite you to continue your journey, then, with courage in heart and reason in hand.

CHAPTER 14

ON THE OTHER SIDE OF THE BRIDGE

YOUR GREAT STORY

This book is for everyone with a kingly nature. I do not write this book merely to tickle your mind or add to your academic library. I write to give your soul a greater vision of the value of your life.

By the light of reason, you are a kingly creature in a great story. Your questions are not a sign of weakness or foolishness. They are a sign of your great purposes on the earth. Your uncertainty is not evidence of the meaninglessness of the world. The entire universe was finely-tuned for people like you to exist and to rise up in the midst of uncertainty.

You are a truth-seeker and a treasure-bringer. The world needs your insights, your ideas, your questions, and your courage. Whether you believe in God or not, you carry treasures for many people.

The foundation of the world is the foundation of your life story. It is the source of all souls, all ideas, and all objects in the universe. It is the source of your mind. It is the source of your breath. It is the treasure within all treasures. The foundation is the king in the midst of all kingly creatures. The foundation fashions the world for heroes, like you.

As long as the foundation exists, you are highly esteemed. You are known. You are valued. Your life has a purpose that precedes you.

If my theory of the foundation were merely an abstract principle, what value would that be to your life? I tell you about the greatest possible treasure because the sight of it is power. Psychologists tell us that those who actively seek and discover value in the world tend to build healthier, happier lives.[1] The perfect foundation contains the greatest concentration of value possible. This foundation has all power, all goodness, and all wisdom. The foundation is eternally stable, always just, and consistently wise. As you see this value, and to the extent that you see it, you gain power to build your life along the lines of your noblest desires.

Your story has only barely begun.

TREASURE LEADS TO MORE TREASURE

In my experience, there is never an end to the discovery of good things. If you find something good, that something can lead to more good. If you have followed the bridge of reason to a great treasure, the journey does not end there. It only begins a new one. From one treasure springs endless more.

In the spirit of exploration, then, on these final pages, I want to leave you with one more thing. It is a special, bonus argument. I give the argument to you as a tool. In your hand, I believe you can use this tool to discover more good things about God.

I present to you the *Argument from Limits*. This argument reveals something about all limits. All properties point to a certain special property, Q, which points to itself. What is Q? The purpose of the Argument from Limits is to reveal the identity of Q. Just as the bridge of reason took us to a foundation of all *things*, the Argument from Limits will take us to a foundation of all *properties*. Reason will be our light.

I start with definitions that lay a foundation for clarity:

D1: A property P is *instantiated*=P characterizes something. (Example: the property *blue* characterizes my shirt, and so blue is instantiated.)

D2: A property P is *explicable*=There could be—without contradicting any principle of reason—an explanation of P's instantiation that does not appeal to P itself. (Example: a factory could have produced the first blue shirts, which explains how the property *being a blue shirt* came to characterize anything.)

D3: A property P is a *limit*=Necessarily, whatever has P is limited in some positive respect. (Example: *being incapable of thinking coherently* is a limit.)

---

[1] See A. L. Duckworth, "Positive Psychology in Clinical Practice," *Annual Review of Clinical Psychology* 1 (2005): 629-51.

For ease of presentation, I will add a technical detail to this definition. I add that limits do not also contain non-limits. To illustrate, *being incapable of thinking and being powerful* conceptually contains a non-limit, *being powerful*. Here, the property is a *mix* of a limit with a non-limit. For our purposes, I will not count such mixes as true limits. To be precise, then, limits are *pure limits*—that is, without non-limits inside.

Now for the secret argument:

1. Every limit is explicable.
2. The property, having limits, is itself a limit.
3. Therefore, having limits is explicable. (1, 2)
4. If having limits is explicable, something could lack limits.
5. Therefore, something could lack limits. (3, 4)
6. If something could lack limits, then something must be perfect.
7. Therefore, something must be perfect (i.e., God). (5, 6)

To help you enter this argument, I will offer a few thoughts to clarify and motivate each premise:

1. Every limit is explicable. This step is about *logically consistent* explanations. For example, the limited size of the earth has a consistent (and *actual*) explanation in terms of the forces that produced the earth. When I say the explanation is "consistent," I mean that no principle of reason—that is, truth of logic (what you can sense by reason)—contradicts the possibility of an explanation.

I propose two ways to check the truth of (1). First, use reason. By reason, I predict you can always conceive of *some* explanation of limits. That is, for any limit L, you can coherently theorize that something prior to L's instantiation produced something with L. If I'm right, then you can enjoy reason-based evidence for (1).

The second check is by observation: you observe many explanations of many limits, and (1) makes good sense of your observations. You might think, moreover, that differences in mere limits cannot be relevant to a difference in explicability.

To be especially modest and careful, one could treat (1) as a *rule of thumb*. The idea here is that if you take any limit, then you can at least expect there to be some possible explanation of that limit, other things being equal. Compare: if you doubted that *gravity* applies to some particular rocks on some random planet, I assume you would have some reason to motivate your doubts in this particular case. In the same way, I propose that if someone doubts the explicability of limits applies to some particular limit, then that person would—or should—have some reason to motivate the exception. In the absence of such a reason, one is free to treat each limit alike as explicable.

2. The property, having limits, is itself a limit. By our definition (D3), having limits certainly counts as a limit: trivially, whatever has *limits* is limited. Hence, premise (2) follows by definition.

3. Therefore, having limits is explicable. This step follows from (1) and (2). The logic behind the inference is universal instantiation: (1) every A is B; (2) X is A; therefore, (3) X is B.

4. If having limits is explicable, something could lack limits. When I use the term *explicable*, I intend to talk about a *non-circular* explanation (according to the intended definition). In other words, the explanation of X cannot be solely in terms of X. For this reason, the explanation of *limited* things cannot be solely in terms of *limited* things. The full explanation of limited things—of why *having limits* is instantiated at all—can only be in terms of something that is not limited. This result follows by my definition of "explicable."

5. Therefore, something could lack limits. This step follows from (3) and (4). The logic behind the inference is modus ponens: (1) A (2) if A, then B; (3) therefore, B.

6. If something could lack limits, then something is perfect. This step is about the logic of perfection. By definition, only something *perfect* could lack limits. Whatever is less than perfect has some limit in some positive respect, whereas whatever is perfect is *purely positive*—and so has no limits in any positive respect. For this reason, perfection would provide a terminus for explanations: by its pure positivity, perfection includes perfect, ultimate, and necessary existence. (See chapter eleven, Perfect Foundation.)

We can now deduce a key consequence: the only way perfection *could* be instantiated is if perfection is *necessarily instantiated* (because the necessary instantiation of perfection is part of perfection). I give a technical deduction below. In other words, either perfection is impossible, or it is necessary. Putting these pieces together, we reach the sixth step: if something could lack limits (i.e., be perfect), then something must be perfect.

Going Deeper

Here I will give a technical deduction in the "S5 logic" of possibility. I will start with definitions. Let the symbols "◊" and "□" abbreviate "possibly" (i.e., consistent with the principles of reason) and "necessarily" (i.e., not possibly not), respectively. The symbol "¬" abbreviates negation (or "not"). Finally, let "P" = "perfection is instantiated."

We now deduce P from ◊P as follows:

1. Let Q = ¬P.
2. If ◊Q, then □◊Q. (By Axiom 5 of S5, that whatever is possible cannot be impossible.)
3. If ◊¬P, then □◊¬P. (By definition of Q.)
4. If ◊¬P, then ¬◊¬◊¬P. (By definition of "□.")
5. If ¬¬◊¬◊¬P, then ¬◊¬P. (By contraposition.)
6. If ◊¬◊¬P, then ¬◊¬P. (By double negation.)
7. If ◊□P, then □P. (By definition of "□.")
8. If ◊P, then P. (By □P ↔ P.)

For anyone who might be unsure about the correctness of S5 logic, I invite you to treat axiom 5 as constituting an implicit definition of the term "possible" in this context.[2] Then you will be reading this argument in its best light.

---

[2]We can illustrate this definition of "possible" in terms of possible worlds. Let us say that the Ws are all possible worlds. If axiom 5 is true, then all the Ws would be possible (consistent with reason) no matter which of the Ws were to obtain. But suppose some of the Ws would not be possible were certain other of the Ws to obtain. Put those aside. Let "possible world" only refer to worlds that have the same principles of reason that hold in our world (i.e., the law of noncontradiction, the law that prime numbers cannot be prime ministers, and so on). Then, by definition, all possible worlds remain possible (consistent with reason) no matter which of these possible worlds obtains.

7. Therefore, something is perfect (i.e., God). This final step follows from (5) and (6). (The logic behind this inference is again modus ponens.)

This argument is a lot to digest. Feel free to retrace the steps. Assess them. Test them. See if they can unlock any additional insights. Take what adds value to you. Leave the rest.

Here is my big-picture summary. By the steps above, properties point back to their ultimate explanation. The ultimate explanation of *limits* cannot be in terms of limits (for that would be circular). Therefore, the ultimate explanation of limits can only be in terms of something without limits. Enter perfection. Perfection is the one property that entails its own *ultimacy*. Perfection is the one property that can be instantiated prior to all others. In this way, all other properties point back to perfection.

To close these final pages, I'd like to share one more idea with you, just for fun. I have an idea about how perfection may *point to itself*. The philosopher Anselm hinted at this way when he famously argued for God from the definition of "perfection" (i.e., "that than which nothing greater can be conceived").[3] Unfortunately, his hints were not sufficiently precise. They left philosophers—myself among them—without clear sight. Philosophers have echoed, "You cannot define God into existence."[4]

Yet the story is not over. In the twentieth century, logicians have supplied new resources for clarifying the logic of perfection.[5] Now, at this place in human history, I think I might see a way to clarify how perfection could point to itself.

I am going to present a *key* just for you. I believe this key can unlock the logic of perfection. The key is in the *nature of perfection*.

When we reflect on pure perfection, we can see that perfection *itself* has positive properties. For example, perfection has *uniqueness*, *greatness*, and *ultimacy*. The positivity of perfection is the key.

Before I propose how to use the key, let us be sure we take the right key in hand. It is easy to mistake the intended key for fake keys nearby. For example, some people have tried to use this key: perfection *entails* (or *includes*) positive features. Some have instead tried to work with the

---

[3]Anselm, *Proslogion* (Indianapolis: Hackett, 2001).

[4]For recent assessments and developments, see G. Oppy, ed., *Ontological Arguments* (Cambridge: Cambridge University Press, 2018), which includes J. Rasmussen, "Plantinga's Ontological Argument," 176-94.

[5]J. Garson, *Modal Logic for Philosophers*, 2nd ed. (Cambridge: Cambridge University Press, 2016).

concept of perfection. Don't take these keys. They unlock nothing for us except parodies.[6]

To see the right key, I propose we look *through* the lens of the concept of perfection. See a *perfect nature*. See its positivity.[7]

There are two things to notice next, both of which point to the same special thing. First, the perfect nature has a *simplicity*. Perfection is a basic, undivided nature (from which other properties—like perfect power, perfect wisdom, and so on—*follow*). Perfection is not like complex properties, such as *big and tall* or *square and circular*. Complex properties have more "opportunity" to be inconsistent, since they have multiple pieces that could exclude one another. A square circle, for example, is composed of multiple properties, *square* and *circle*, which exclude each other. While complex properties can be consistent, they can also fail to be consistent. A simple nature, by contrast, has no pieces that could exclude others. Hence, simplicity points to a special property: *logical consistency* (i.e., consistence with reason).[8]

Here is something else to notice: if we can indeed see the positivity of the perfect nature (of perfection), then by further reflection, perhaps we can see that the perfect nature is the most positive of any nature. It is the greatest nature. This greatness is a second witness to logical consistency: the greatest nature is consistent because inconsistence is negative (not positive) and detracts from a nature's greatness. In this way, the *perfect* nature points—by the twin lights of simplicity and positivity—to its consistency.

We now have the key. We can insert this key into a recent system of logic. Here is what I mean: by developments in the logic of possibility, philosophers discovered that *if* perfection is *possibly* instantiated (i.e., consistent with reason), then perfection *must be* instantiated (see the previous Going Deeper section for the details). In view of this discovery, we might now ask, "Why think perfection is *possibly* instantiated?"[9]

---

[6]For example, while perfection may *include* or *entail* necessary existence, so does *being a necessarily existent island*. Nothing helpful follows.

[7]A. Pruss, "A Gödelian Ontological Argument Improved," *Religious Studies* 45, no. 3 (2009): 347-53 works with this same key. I have a slightly different way to turn it.

[8]While I suspect *all* simple, unified natures are consistent (because they have no pieces that could exclude each other), to be modest, I propose here that, other things being equal, simplicity is a reason to expect consistency.

[9]See Oppy, ed., *Ontological Arguments*, 182.

Here is an idea: *perfection—by the light of its simplicity and positivity—points to its own possibility (i.e., consistency).* Something cool follows: by the logic of possibility, perfection must be instantiated. In this way, perfection points, *by its own nature*, to its instantiation. As far as I can tell, no other property is like that.

The system is now complete: all properties point to perfection, either by pointing back to perfection (by the Argument from Limits) or by pointing to itself—via its positivity. If the system works, then all properties of all things point to God.

BIBLIOGRAPHY

Anselm. *Proslogion*. Indianapolis: Hackett, 2001.

Aquinas, T. *Summa theologiae*. Translated by Fathers of the English Dominican Province. New York: Benzinger, 1948.

Aristotle. *Metaphysics*. Translated by Joe Sachs. New Mexico: Green Lion Press, 2002.

Beauregard, M., and D. O'Leary. *The Spiritual Brain: A Neuroscientist's Case for the Existence of the Soul*. San Francisco: HarperOne, 2008.

Byerly, R. "From a Necessary Being to a Perfect Being." *Analysis* 9 (2018): 10-17.

Chalmers, D. "Facing Up to the Problem of Consciousness." *Journal of Consciousness Studies* 2, no. 3 (1995): 200-219.

Churchland, Patricia. *Neurophilosophy: Toward a Unified Science of the Mind/Brain*. Cambridge, MA: MIT Press, 1986.

Churchland, Paul. *A Neurocomputational Perspective*. Cambridge, MA: MIT Press, 1989.

Collins, R. "God, Design, and Fine-Tuning." In *God Matters: Readings in the Philosophy of Religion*, edited by R. M. Bernard, 54-65. London: Longman, 2003.

Colyvan, M. *An Introduction to the Philosophy of Math*. Cambridge: Cambridge University Press, 2012.

Copleston, F. C., and B. Russell. "A Debate on the Existence of God." BBC. 1948. www.scandalon.co.uk/philosophy/cosmological_radio.htm.

Craig, W. L. "Can a Loving God Send People to Hell? The Craig-Bradley Debate." Simon Fraser University, 1994. www.reasonablefaith.org/media/debates/can-a-loving-god-send-people-to-hell-the-craig-bradley-debate/.

Davidson, M. "God and Other Necessary Beings." *Stanford Encyclopedia of Philosophy.* 2013. https://plato.stanford.edu/entries/god-necessary-being/.

Dawkins, R. *The God Delusion*. New York: Houghton Mifflin, 2006.

DeRose, K. "Universalism and the Bible." https://campuspress.yale.edu/keithderose/.

Dougherty, T., and A. Pruss. "Evil and the Problem of Anomaly." *Oxford Studies in Philosophy of Religion* 5 (2014): 49-87.

Dougherty, T. *The Problem of Animal Pain: A Theodicy for All Creatures Great and Small.* New York: Palgrave, 2014.

Duckworth, A. L. "Positive Psychology in Clinical Practice." *Annual Review of Clinical Psychology* 1 (2005): 629-51.

Edwards, P. "The Cosmological Argument." In *The Rationalist Annual for the Year*, edited by C. Watts, 63-77. London: Pemberton, 1959.

Freddoso, A. J., and T. Flint. "Maximal Power." *The Existence and Nature of God*, edited by A. J. Freddoso, 81-113. Notre Dame: University of Notre Dame Press, 1983.

Garson, J. *Modal Logic for Philosophers*. 2nd ed. Cambridge: Cambridge University Press, 2016.

Gozzano, S., and C. S. Hill, eds. *New Perspectives on Type Identity*. Cambridge: Cambridge University Press, 2012.

Harman, G. "Ethics and Observation." In *Ethical Theory 1: The Question of Objectivity*, edited by J. Rachels, 85-91. Oxford: Oxford University Press, 1998.

Harris, S. *The Moral Landscape: How Science Can Determine Human Values*. New York: Free Press, 2011.

Hasker, W. *The Emergent Self.* Ithaca, NY: Cornell University Press, 1999.

Hawking, S. *A Brief History of Time*. New York: Bantam, 1988.

Henderson, L. "The Problem of Induction." *Stanford Encyclopedia of Philosophy* 2018. https://plato.stanford.edu/entries/induction-problem/.

Huemer, M. *Ethical Intuitionism*. New York: Palgrave, 2005.

Hume, D. *Dialogues Concerning Natural Religion*. Cambridge: Cambridge University Press, 2007 (also 1779).

Kant, I. *The Critique of Pure Reason*. Translated and edited by Paul Guyer and Allen Wood. Cambridge: Cambridge University Press, 1998.

Koons, R. "A New Look at the Cosmological Argument." *American Philosophical Quarterly* 34 (1997): 193-212.

Leibniz, G. "On the Ultimate Origin of Things." In *Discourse on Metaphysics and Other Essays*. Indianapolis: Hackett, 1991.

Lewis, C. S. *The Problem of Pain*. New York: Harper Collins, 1940.

———. *The Great Divorce*. New York: Harper Collins, 1946.

———. *Mere Christianity*. New York: Harper Collins, 1952.

———. *The Last Battle*. New York: Harper Collins, 1956.

Lightman, A. "The Accidental Universe." *Harper's*. December 2011. https://harpers.org/archive/2011/12/the-accidental-universe/.

Mackie, J. L. "Evil and Omnipotence." *Mind* LXIV, no. 254 (1955): 200-212.

K. M. Masters, and G. Spielmans. "Prayer and Health: Review, Meta-Analysis, and Research Agenda." *Journal of Behavioral Medicine* 30 (2007): 329-38.

Merricks, T. *Objects and Persons*. Oxford: Oxford University Press, 2001.

More, P. E. *Platonism*. London: Princeton University Press, 1917.

Morriston, W. "What Is So Good about Moral Freedom." *Philosophical Quarterly* 50 (2000): 344-358.

Nozick, R. *Anarchy, State, and Utopia*. New York: Basic Books, 1974.

Oddie, G. *Value, Reality, and Desire*. New York: Oxford University Press, 2005.

Oppy, G. "Omnipotence." *Philosophy and Phenomenological Research* 71, no. 1 (2005): 58-84.

———, *Describing Gods*. Cambridge: Cambridge University Press, 2014.

———, ed. *Ontological Arguments*. Cambridge: Cambridge University Press, 2018.

Plantinga, A. *God, Freedom, and Evil*. Grand Rapids: Eerdmans, 1974.

———. *Nature of Necessity*. New York: Oxford University Press, 1974.

Pearce, K., and A. Pruss. "Understanding Omnipotence." *Religious Studies* 48, no. 3 (2012): 403-14.

Pruss, A. *The Principle of Sufficient Reason*. New York: Cambridge University Press, 2006.

———. "A Gödelian Ontological Argument Improved." *Religious Studies* 45, no. 3 (2009): 347-53.

Pruss, A., and J. Rasmussen. *Necessary Existence*. New York: Oxford University Press, 2018.

Quine, W. V. O. "On What There Is." *The Review of Metaphysics* 2, no. 5 (1948): 21-38.

———. "Quantifiers and Propositional Attitudes." *The Journal of Philosophy* 53, no. 5 (1956): 177-87.

Ramsey, W. "Eliminative Materialism." *Stanford Encyclopedia of Philosophy*. 2013. https://plato.stanford.edu/entries/materialism-eliminative/.

Rasmussen, J. "From a Necessary Being to God." *Religious Studies* 66, no. 1 (2009): 1-13.

———. "On the Value of the Freedom to Do Evil." *Faith and Philosophy* 30 (2013): 418-28.

———. "Building Thoughts from Dust: A Cantorian Puzzle." *Synthese* 192 (2015): 393-404.

———. "Plantinga's Ontological Argument." In *Ontological Arguments*, edited by G. Oppy, 176-94. Cambridge: Cambridge University Press, 2018.

———. "Against Non-Reductive Physicalism." In *The Blackwell Companion to Substance Dualism*, edited by Jonathan J. Loose, Angus J. L. Menuge, and J. P. Moreland, 328–39. Malden, MA: Wiley-Blackwell, 2018.

Rota, M. *Taking Pascal's Wager: Faith, Evidence, and the Abundant Life*. Downers Grove, IL: InterVarsity Press, 2016.

Rowe, W. *The Cosmological Argument*. Princeton: Princeton University Press, 1975.

Russell, B. *Principles of Mathematics*. Cambridge: Cambridge University Press, 1903.

Scotus, D. *Duns Scotus: Philosophical Writings*. Indianapolis: Hackett, 1987.

Searle, J. *Mind: A Brief Introduction*. Oxford: Oxford University Press, 2005.

Schaffer, J. "Monism." *Stanford Encyclopedia of Philosophy*. 2018. https://plato.stanford.edu/entries/monism/.

Schellenberg, J. *The Hiddenness Argument: Philosophy's New Challenge to Belief in God*. New York: Oxford University Press, 2015.

Schwartz, J. M., and S. Begley. *The Mind and the Brain: Neuroplasticity and the Power of Mental Force*. New York: Harper Collins, 2002.

Speaks, J. *The Greatest Possible Being*. Oxford: Oxford University Press, 2018.

Spinoza, B. *Ethics*. Edited by Matthew J. Kisner. Translated by Michael Silverthorne. Cambridge: Cambridge University Press, 2018.

Stitch, S. *Deconstructing the Mind*. New York: Oxford University Press, 1996.

Swinburne, R. *The Christian God*. Oxford: Oxford University Press, 1994.

———. *Providence and the Problem of Evil*. Oxford: Clarendon, 1998.

Talbott, T. *The Inescapable Love of God*. 2nd ed. Eugene, OR: Cascade, 2014.

Tegmark, M. *Our Mathematical Universe: My Quest for the Ultimate Nature of Reality*. New York: Random House, 2014.

Timmons, M. *Moral Theory: An Introduction*. Lanham, MD: Rowman & Littlefield, 2013.

Tooley, M. "The Problem of Evil." *Stanford Encyclopedia of Philosophy*. 2015. https://plato.stanford.edu/entries/evil/.

Uebel, T. "Vienna Circle." *Stanford Encyclopedia of Philosophy*. 2014. https://plato.stanford.edu/entries/vienna-circle/.

Van Inwagen, P. *Material Beings*. Ithaca, NY: Cornell University Press, 1990.

———. *The Problem of Evil*. Oxford: Oxford University Press, 2006.

———. *An Essay on Free Will*. Oxford: Clarendon, 1983.

———. "Meta-Ontology." *Erkenntnis* 48, nos. 2-3 (1998): 233-50.

Wagner, A. *Solving Evolution's Greatest Puzzle*. New York: Penguin, 2014.

Walls, J. *Purgatory: The Logic of Total Transformation*. Oxford: Oxford University Press, 2012.

Wessling, and J. Rasmussen. "Reasons for Randomness." *Theology and Science* 13, no. 3 (2015): 288-304.

Wykstra, S. "Rowe's Noseeum Arguments from Evil." In *The Evidential Argument from Evil*, edited by D. Howard-Snyder, 126-50. Bloomington: Indiana University Press, 1996.

INDEX